THE NEW:BUNGALOW:

ESSAYS BY MATTHEW BIALECKI, AIA

CHRISTIAN GLADU

JILL KESSENICH, ASSOCIATE AIA

JIM MCCORD, AIA

SU BACON

Gibbs Smith, Publisher
TO ENRICH AND INSPIRE HUMANKIND
Salt Lake City | Charleston | Santa Fe | Santa Barbara

12 11 10 09 08   5 4 3 2 1

First printed in hardbound edition 2001 by Gibbs Smith, Publisher

Published by

Gibbs Smith, Publisher

P.O. Box 667

Layton, Utah 84041

1-800.835.4993 orders

www.gibbs-smith.com

Cover designed and produced by Traci O'Very Covey

Interior designed and produced by FORTHGEAR, Inc.

Printed and bound in China

Library of Congress Cataloging-in-Publication Data

Bialecki, Matthew.

  The new bungalow / essays by Matthew Bialecki, Christian Gladu, Jill Kessenich, Jim McCord, and Su Bacon.—1st ed.

        p. cm.

  ISBN 10: 1-58685-042-3 (hb); 1-4236-0435-0 (pb)

  ISBN 13: 978-1-4236-0435-8 (pb)

  1. Bungalows—Unites States—History. 2. Architecture—United States—20th century. 3. Arts and Crafts Movement—Influence. I. Gladu, Christian. II. Kessenich, Jill. III. McCord, Jim. IV. Bacon, Su.

V. Title.

  NA7571.B53 2001

  728.'373—dc21

2001002766

Contents

Introduction   1

Origins of the Bungalow   4

Elements of Bungalow Style   32

Renovation: Where to Start?   44

The New Bungalow Revival   58

Interpreting the Spirit   128

Home Show of Details   140

Resources   150

Photo Credits   155

Acknowledgments

Our deepest thanks to the following individuals and companies who helped us round out our understanding of the bungalow in today's architecture and who shared information, philosophy, leads, and photographs, and some of whom opened their homes for photographing:

Tim Ashmore

Su Bacon

Matthew Bialecki

John Brinkmann

Marshall Compton

Mikel Covey

Traci O'Very Covey

Brett Gee

Curtis Gelotte

Christian Gladu

Christen Gladu

Lee Hershberger

Don Hensman

Ted Houseknecht

Valerie Johnson

Jill Kessenich

Lis King

Lynn King

Robert Lidsky

Johan Luchsinger

Randell L. Makinson

John Malick

Michael and Jane Mangelson

Jim McCord

Alex Moseley

David Papazian

Voorhees Craftsman

Robert Winter

Introduction

For three decades, Gibbs Smith, Publisher, has been exploring the works of Greene & Greene, Bernard Maybeck, and Frank Lloyd Wright. But the truth is that very few of us can own a masterpiece like the Greenes' ultimate bungalow, or a house of the quality of Wright—but we can afford a home in a style that moves beyond nationwide suburban and tract homes and condominium complexes that all look the same. Where can the sameness end and individual expression begin? It begins with *The New Bungalow*.

We have watched American taste for retro style and antiques move old-home renovation to an unprecedented level of popularity and taste, and have witnessed a marked demand for information on remodeling and decorating bungalow homes. They fit right in with a taste for things of the past; their smallness appeals for its manageability. Even though most people have never lived in one, they long for the neighborhood homes like those in which their parents and grandparents lived.

To many Arts & Crafts enthusiasts, bungalows are about a narrowly defined style, a certain look. The truth of the matter is that bungalows exist throughout the country in a variety of different styles. This book shows examples of homes that run the gamut from pure classical to the more interpretive designs. Yet all of them exude the true spirit of the bungalow—architectural expressions of a philosophy that took hold a century and a half ago.

Homes showcased within also run the gamut in affordability. Some of them focus on simplicity and efficient use of space. Others are high-end dwellings with thousands of square feet and utilizing pricey materials. At both ends of the spectrum—whether the house is in the $80 or $800-per-square-foot range—builders and owners have treated themselves to details that will last for generations, such as tile fireplace surrounds, doors and windows with character and class, and attractive and functional built-in cabinets and benches. Whether your budget is $80 or $800 a square foot, there are ideas and creative solutions here that will expand and enrich your understanding of the bungalow as a housing type for today's lifestyle.

After having read architects' and historians' educated opinions on the bungalow and its place in the past and today, foremost in our minds were the questions "What is a bungalow?" "What is its appeal?" "Why are we drawn to this style of house?" "In what ways is it appropriate for today's lifestyle?" To get some answers, we looked to the architects and builders who are creating new bungalows, to some who are remodeling old bungalows, and to the past for the principles underlying the original Arts & Crafts movement.

In our research, we called upon some experts: Randell L. Makinson, Hon. AIA, scholar and author of numerous books on Greene and Greene, their homes, and their distinctive architectural style; Robert Winter, art and architectural historian and author of books on the American bungalow as well as Batchelder tiles and architectural guidebooks to Los Angeles and San Francisco. Both Makinson and Winter led us to people whose philosophies and works are featured in this book. We also searched the Internet and were elated to find a number of architects in various regions of the country offering new plans for bungalow homes and bungalow neighborhoods.

Then we began dialogues with the architects and designers themselves. It was exhilarating to learn firsthand their various approaches to the modern bungalow, their interpretations of its elements, style, and materials. Their enthusiasm made it obvious that each of the professionals whose writings, photographs, and designs appear in this book is fully engaged in developing a house style for people today. They are keen on quality and allocation of space; they are tuned in to the environment both aesthetically and from an ecological standpoint; they are champions of the bungalow revival and are steadily enlisting disciples.

Matthew Bialecki, AIA, of Matthew Bialecki Associates, New Paltz, New York, has possibly the broadest interpretation of those architects and designers whose essays are included in this book. He analyzes the philosophy of the original Arts & Crafts movement that started in the mid-1800s in England and shows how the American Arts & Crafts proponents carried the tenets along. He strongly advocates nature-based design as the answer for twenty-first-century residential architecture.

Christian Gladu of The Bungalow Company in Bend, Oregon, has developed bungalow neighborhoods with life and vitality on Bainbridge Island, Washington, and other locations. His designs integrate the style and timeless charm of the past with a modern point of view. Gladu helps us understand the quality of life that can be achieved through bungalow living and illustrates how the bungalow style has adapted to fit the needs of today's homeowners.

Jill Kessenich, Associate AIA, is a partner with Tim Ashmore in Ashmore/Kessenich Design with offices in Madison, Wisconsin, and Portland, Oregon. They specialize in house designs inspired by the early twentieth century. Kessenich shares professional advice on restoring old bungalows, and examples of their designs provide fresh options for new-home construction in the classic style.

Jim McCord, AIA, of Monterey, California, shares some practical advice on ways to achieve a bungalow look and feel in a remodel or spec home, detailing construction elements that can be upgraded or simply selected with prudence by the homeowner to achieve a bungalow look.

Su Bacon, interior and lighting designer and co-owner of Historic Lighting in Monrovia, California, has outfitted historic remodels of Greene & Greene, new homes in the style of the Greenes, and many other historic residences and businesses with period-appropriate lighting. She shares her design professional's perspective on the function of lighting in today's homes and addresses each aspect: sconces, ceiling lights, lamps, and makes a case for the use of the newer recessed lighting technology in the bungalow.

Numerous additional architects, interior designers, and homeowners have opened their archives and homes, lending photographs for this book and allowing new photography as well. To them, we are deeply appreciative. A few architects who we wished to include were unable to participate for one reason or another, some having to do with privacy wishes of the homeowners. Nevertheless, we have listed their firms in the Resources, as we recognize their driving efforts in the bungalow revival.

We have been enlightened through our interaction with each individual and firm that is represented in this book. We trust that you will be inspired as well. —*The Editors*

OF THE
: ORIGINS BUNGALOW :

Matthew Bialecki, AIA

New bungalows can be made, new objects created; but if they are to be as valued and treasured as the originals we admire, they need to do more than copy the look: they need to interpret the original spirit and objectives for our time and place.

Matthew Bialecki, AIA

Could anyone have predicted in the early 1920s, when the original Arts & Crafts movement died out, that it would enjoy a revival that would start some fifty years later and last longer than the original movement? Arts & Crafts has evolved into a national style phenomenon. It is now possible to live in Arts & Crafts–themed developments, work in Arts & Crafts–inspired office parks, eat in Arts & Crafts–styled restaurants and, of course, buy most any Arts & Crafts–style furniture at your local mall, big-box retailer,

Maclucas house in Pacific Palisades, California. This craftsman remodel was first done in the mid-1980s. Courtesy of Historic Lighting.

5

The tall tree-like posts blend the house with the surrounding woods. Gundlach House, New Paltz, New York, Matthew Bialecki, architect.

or Web site. What happened to our obscure, little, cognoscente-only art movement that turned it into a multi-media merchandising juggernaut?

With the revival now well into its fourth decade, it is time to pause and critically ask what is fueling this great interest in a minor hundred-year-old art movement. Where is the bungalow revival going, and, more importantly, will it support a new architecture and a new way of living?

Front elevation, Studley residence, Gardiner, New York, Matthew Bialecki, architect.

The answer lies in understanding the principles of the original architects and artists who founded the movement in the nineteenth century. To be sure, there will always be a market for the fine and rare artifacts of any notable period, but that audience is limited and the marketing activity is ultimately commercial, not creative. New bungalows can be made, new objects created; but if they are to be as valued and treasured as the originals we admire, they need to do more than copy the look: they need to interpret the original spirit and objectives for our time and place. A review of those principles will lay the groundwork for interpreting the bungalow for our time.

A Brief History

Many people who are just becoming acquainted with the style today would be astonished at how quickly the original American Arts & Crafts and bungalow movement came and went. It was barely sixteen years from Stickley's introduction of his first craftsman furniture (1900) and the first printing of his magazine, *The Craftsman.*

An early California bungalow shows the typical overhanging eaves and exposed structure. It is blended nicely with the landscape for a unified design.

An early rear view of the Blacker House, designed by Charles and Henry Greene.

Charles and Henry Greene, the greatest architects of the bungalow movement and designers of the finest bungalows, didn't fare much better. They started their practice in Pasadena in 1894, gradually developing their art and business until reaching the apex of their careers in 1910, when they completed the last of their five "ultimate bungalows." They built significant work for another eight years but, nevertheless,

from that pinnacle they slowly but steadily faded until in 1922 they dissolved their firm. A mere twenty-five years had elapsed from tentative beginnings to acknowledged masterworks to professional obscurity.

Were design tastes so fickle? How could something that now seems so timeless and enduring have faded so quickly?

In the early 1900s, companies made the style available to anyone by delivering bungalow kits to one's doorstep.

The great bungalow building boom of the 1910s and '20s was the popular acknowledgement of Stickley's and the Greenes' accomplishments, but it eventually became a victim of its own success. With factories delivering bungalow kits to your doorstep and builders creating bungalow heavens coast to coast by the score, the original qualities that made them so popular got lost. By the late '20s and '30s, the bungalow had became a synonym for "cheap little house."

But what cheap little houses! Porches, woodwork, built-ins, windows—who could resist? It is easy to see why the bungalows were so popular: they provided a traditional sense of craftsmanship in a fundamentally contemporary home. Simply, bungalows were America's first popular example of modern architecture, and we loved it. In fact, bungalows and their progeny—the ranch house of the 1940s–60s—were the dominant housing type for the twentieth century.

Bungalows in all varieties of shapes and sizes were advertised across the country as the answer to housing needs after World War II.

What elements made them so popular?

- The compact plan merged front hall and parlor, creating an open, flowing space.

- The homes were mostly one story and volumetrically horizontal.

- The windows were large and mostly horizontally proportioned, making bungalows bright and transparent.

- The wood structure was exposed and celebrated, even exaggerated, with beams, rafter tails, and structural framing details highlighted as decorations.

- The bungalow house was linked to the yard and garden.

In the finest examples of American Arts & Crafts architecture—Greene and Greene's ultimate bungalows— the houses are inseparable from the gardens. The entire scope of house and environment is conceived as one intrinsic design. Terraces embrace porches, which flow into living spaces filled with materials and images from the garden. Sleeping porches, balconies, and courtyards dissolve the "built" architecture into the landscape. With the doors open on a summer night, you don't know if you are inside or out. The ultimate bungalows are much more a pavilion in the landscape than a house next to a garden. Even at the most modest scale, the bungalows have the porch and the garden that maintain the feel of a pavilion.

The bungalow was the design for America's new millennium. A new plan, a new look, a new lifestyle. Yes, it's heretical to say anything about contemporary architecture among history-soaked, fumed-oak, clinker-bricked, open-beamed bungalow fanatics, but it's true: bungalows were America's first widely available modern architecture and we have never looked back. The bungalow craze of the teens and '20s never really ended. It was just given a different name—the ranch.

One reason bungalows became popular was that they celebrated their wood structure by using structural framing details as decorations.

Art historians have long recognized that significant artistic movements follow an almost predictable trajectory from discovery ➢ achievement ➢ gradual decline into obscurity ➢ eventual rediscovery and reinvention. Clearly, the current bungalow revival is our rediscovery and reinvention phase. This is truly a renaissance of ideas and not just images with origins in the English Arts & Crafts movement. The fundamental principles of the American bungalow were developed in England in the mid-nineteenth century, and the aspirations of those original artists and architects are the basis for the ideals of the new bungalow renaissance.

England 1840–90

While the American bungalow movement followed the historical cycle of discovery through decline from 1900–30, the Arts & Crafts movement in England began its trajectory about fifty years earlier.

Up until that time, English architecture was centered completely on accepted historical styles—Greek, Roman, French Renaissance, Baroque, Gothic, Romanesque, Moorish, and so forth. Debates among architects became increasingly narrow and the issues more obscure: Parish churches should definitely be Gothic! Government buildings can only be Greek! Meanwhile, the industrial revolution had developed new technologies (steel frames, glass walls, mass production of components) that were rarely acknowledged.

The leading English architects were filled with uncertainty about the practicality of the historical styles. Buildings other than palaces and churches were needed—train stations, offices, warehouses—to which historic styles often didn't conform. By mid-century, the stage had been readied for the two great struggles of twentieth-century architectural theory: Nature and the Machine, or "bungalow vs. Bauhaus."

Designed by architect John Malick, the Cereghino home recalls the charming, unpretentious homes of nineteenth-century British architect C. F .A. Voysey.

PUGIN, RUSKIN, MORRIS: NATURE-BASED ARCHITECTURE

By the time of his premature death in 1852 at the age of forty, Augustus Welby Pugin was already recognized as the savior of English architecture. His work on the Houses of Parliament with Charles Barry had crowned an extraordinary career as an architect and designer. Although he was primarily considered for his work in the Gothic Revival, he was widely read and praised for his advocacy of a return to the craft traditions of the medieval guilds and to an expressive, straightforward approach to exposing structural elements such as beams, stone walls, and hardware.

Pugin turned away from the debate over historical styles and found his own unique expression. His principle of truthfulness—handcrafted materials used honestly and showing the structure of a building directly—would become fundamental principles of the first Arts & Crafts architects two decades later.

Indeed, it is difficult to imagine Pugin's contemporaries—the great critic and theorist John Ruskin, and William Morris, the grandfather of the English Arts & Crafts movement—able to support their theories without having Pugin's work as an example. Ruskin, Morris, and their followers were active critics against the injustices of the industrial revolution. And, like Pugin, they believed that art and architecture had the capacity to redeem and reform society. They lived and wrote in favor of a simple life rejuvenated by the handcrafting of art. Morris rejoiced in the wonders and restorative power of nature, and representations of the natural world filled his art.

The main body of the Cereghino residence has a heavy stucco finish and is detailed to create the appearance of an old stone building.

The Hoelter residence boasts a new garden design, inspired by the English gardens of Gertrude Jekyll, which creates a clearly recognizable pathway from the street to the front entry. John Malick, architect.

Wooden framing in the high ceilings of the Cereghino residence brings warmth and spaciousness to the living room. John Malick, architect.

From the founding of Morris & Company in London in 1861 until Morris's death in 1896, he and his circle were the leading decorative artists and theoretical leaders of the growing Arts & Crafts movement. He redefined art to include traditional crafts such as stained glass, weaving, wallpaper and pattern making, bookbinding, tiles, murals, and furniture design. His designs were not merely objects to admire; they were an integral part of a philosophy that proposed a new lifestyle of self-reliance that celebrated an artistic life. "Have nothing in your houses which you do not know to be useful or believe to be beautiful," he said.

Morris inspired all the great architects of the English Arts & Crafts movement: Webb, Voysey, Lethaby, Lutyens, Ballie Scott, and others. It

Malick redesigned this home with many gardens, gates, and trellises to integrate the house and garden.

was these architects who most successfully implemented Morris's ideals and developed three of the most important aspects of the future bungalow movement: the celebration and use of vernacular architecture (using local natural materials), the unifying of a building's architecture with its interior fixtures and furnishings, and the integration of the house and garden. For example, Lethaby's Melsetter House on Orkney is as vernacular as a group of massive boulders; a home so completely part of the island's building tradition and landscape that it would flounder anywhere else; Voysey's Bormley and Moorcrag houses in Cumbria, with their slate roofs like piles of rocks hovering over whitewashed walls, both contrast with the lush green hills and fit in like a strong crag.

19

The Cereghino residence's staircase is the masterwork of the home.

The interiors were equally radical. Rejecting the fixtures and furnishings produced at the time as hopelessly garish and inappropriate, the English Arts & Crafts architects simply made their own. The Red House by Webb and Morris was considered shockingly bare, a neutral background for the hand-painted furniture and elegantly crafted furnishings they designed for it. Voysey, Scott, and Lutyens were masters at designing and fabricating the hardware, glass, textiles, and furniture that fused the interior with the architectural expression.

The last other major achievement by the English Arts & Crafts architects that would have a profound influence on the bungalow movement was the emphasis on integrating the garden with the home. No one did this better than Ballie Scott, whose small gardens show a practicality and beauty.

Traditional Craftsman construction methods create well-above-average life expectancy for the Hoelter residence. John Malick, architect.

In just over fifty years, the English Arts & Crafts movement had broken from the tired stylistic formulas of the past and developed a new architectural language. They created new forms based on nature and the indigenous, vernacular architecture. They defined a whole new integrated approach to the decorative arts and interior design of their buildings. They linked the house with the landscape and the rooms with the garden directly as one element. They promoted a new lifestyle of living and working artistically with nature as guide and muse.

William Morris's work was eagerly read and discussed on both sides of the Atlantic, especially by an idealistic American furniture maker from upstate New York named Gustav Stickley.

The Hoelters' breakfast room and terrace surrounded by nature is part of the Arts & Crafts ideal.

The Hoelter design emphasizes exposed post-and-beam construction and hand-assembled wainscots, casework, doors, and windows.

This home in Salt Lake City was designed and constructed in the Arts & Crafts style through the collaborative effort of John Shirley (exterior), Juidiith Clawson (interior), and Steve Dubell, project foreman for Doug Knight construction. The overriding desire was to build a new house that would blend with the style of an older bungalow neighborhood.

"*We do not believe in large houses with many rooms elaborately decorated and furnished, for the reason that these seem so essentially an outcome of the artificial conditions that lay such harassing burdens upon modern life. . . . That is why we have from the first planned houses that are based on the big fundamental principles of honesty, simplicity and usefulness. . . .*"

—*Gustav Stickley*

If William Morris can be considered the grandfather of the bungalow movement, certainly Gustav Stickley must be the father. Deeply impressed after his meetings with Voysey and

Stickley's traditional designs merged common sense with good design.

Ashbee in England in 1898, Stickley returned to America a disciple. By 1900, he had introduced his soon-to-be-famous craftsman furniture, and a year later, he began publication of *The Craftsman,* the magazine that brought the designs and lifestyle of the bungalow movement to America.

Stickley was more than a furniture maker. His studio produced over two hundred house plans, offered consulting and design services, and claimed by 1913 that several thousand of his Craftsman homes had been built for a total value of over $20 million! As the

apostle of the Arts & Crafts bungalow, Stickley brought the virtues of affordability and practicality to the ideals of the English Arts & Crafts homes. His designs embraced indigenous building types, extolled the virtues of the garden and outdoor spaces, praised simple, honest materials crafted beautifully, and advanced the necessity of convenience and practicality in a home. Kitchens were designed and discussed with as much care as living rooms. Gardens were for recreation and growing fruits and vegetables.

Furnishings were durable and dignified, made of oak, leather, and hammered copper. He brought the Arts & Crafts ideals to the American middle class, merging common sense and good design.

Of the many styles featured in *The Craftsman*, Stickley clearly embraced the wood-shingled, heavy timbered bungalows of California as the ideal expressions of the bungalow movement. He visited there in 1904 and was deeply impressed by the work of the Greenes.

The meticulous woodwork of this contemporary craftsman home is an enduring tribute to the legacy of Greene & Greene. Studley residence, Gardiner, New York, Matthew Bialecki, architect.

The Blacker house was designed as a seamless extension of its gardens and landscape.

Greene is so clearly the high-water mark of the bungalow movement that discussion of other architects and designers almost seems superfluous. Their five ultimate bungalows—the Blacker, Gamble, Thorsen, Pratt, and Ford Houses—are the best examples of the fusion of architecture, landscape architecture, and the decorative arts America has produced. The ultimate bungalows were designed as seamless extensions of their gardens and the landscape, with the interior furnishings and fixtures complementing the garden and architecture perfectly. The homes embodied the bungalow lifestyle with thoughtful and practical kitchens and domestic conveniences while providing the poetic luxuries of sleeping porches, inglenooks, and terraces. Quite simply, they were masterpieces.

With the completion of the ultimate bungalows and the conclusion of Stickley's *Craftsman* in 1916, the artistic and theoretical development of the bungalow and the Arts & Crafts movement stopped. The masterworks had been achieved, the philosophy written, the recognition given.

The bungalow craze, however, was in full swing. Fueled by the great Florida and California land speculations of the twenties, the economic boom, the growth of the middle class, and the mass-marketing of prefabricated bungalow building kits, companies such as Sears, Alladin, Lewis, and others sold by some estimates more than 100,000 homes by the late 1920s. Bungalows had become big business that would take the Great Depression to it slow down, and, in 1932, a little architectural exhibition called International Style to finish it off.

Bungalows like this one were mass marketed by companies such as Sears, Alladin, Lewis, and others.

2658 – Southern California Winter Home of Mrs. Jas A. Garfield at Pasadena.

By the late 1920s, more than 100,000 bungalows had been built.

The Bungalow vs. the Bauhaus, 1930–70

"Frank Lloyd Wright? Why he was the greatest architect of the 19th Century. . . ."—*Phillip Johnson*

With the opening of the now-famous "International Style" exhibition at the Museum of Modern Art in 1932, the Bauhaus made a grand entrance into the American design and architectural world. Homes were, as architect Le Corbusier stated in 1925, "machines for living."

In fact, the entire modern movement was enthralled with the machine and all its aesthetic possibilities. Use factory manufacturing methods and components! Make walls of glass and steel! Abolish the sloped roof! Buildings should express their machine origins and become abstract sculpture. Buildings should contrast with nature, not blend with it.

This was not an architecture that accepted the romantic, the quaint, or the cozy. The bungalow was yester-day's style, at least if you wanted to graduate from architecture school in the 1950s and '60s.

However, a small group of architects kept developing the concepts that were central to the original bunga-lows. Led by Frank Lloyd Wright, Rudolph Schindler, Harwell Harris, William Wurster, and others, architects in the '30s, '40s and '50s talked about architecture inspired by nature, using natural materials. This was the next evolution of the Arts & Crafts movement.

Now, it is true that these new bungalows didn't quite resemble the Stickley/Greene & Greene craftsmans of the 1910s–20s. They were lighter and architecturally more dynamic, but the principles were there— integrating the landscape with the building, exposing the structure, composing the building with horizontal volumes and glass, an overreaching practicality for solving domestic solutions, and a love for wood.

The post-war period was a fertile one for architecture in America. Frank Lloyd Wright's Usonian houses, William Wurster and Joseph Eshrick's emerging Bay Area style, and Harris's many buildings all showed a new way of building with nature. The movement was growing, and it attracted its share of critics.

In 1948 Jean Bangs, Harris's wife and an architectural historian, wrote a series of articles on Greene & Greene and Bernard Maybeck (their contemporary in the Bay Area) that are credited with the "re-discovery and recognition of these [at the time] forgotten architects." At the same time, the debate between the Bauhaus-trained architects and the naturalists reached a boiling point. The famous modernist Marcel Breuer summed up the modernists' disdain for the emerging group of regional, nature-based architects: "I don't feel too much impulse to set 'human' [in the best sense of the word] against formal. If human is considered identical with redwood all over the place, or if it is considered identical with camouflaging architecture with planting, with nature, with romantic subsidies, I am against it."

The debates of the late '40s and early '50s clearly didn't change much among the practitioners. However, it did get a lot of press at House Beautiful, where the influential editor Elizabeth Gordon championed Wright and the whole movement. She published and promoted the nature-based designers and moved readers toward a natural, humanized modernism. The final model of the bungalow was now at hand: the post-war ranch house.

Like the mass-produced bungalows of the '20s had broken the hearts of Greene & Greene, so did the mass-produced versions of Wright's and Harris's houses grieve them. Fueled by the post-war boom, developers stripped the wood, the glass, the nature, and the detail and built the ranch house coast to coast: suburbia was born.

The Arts & Crafts Revival: A New Beginning

By the mid-1970s architects rarely designed work that required a lot of detailed craftsmanship. "They just don't make them like they used to," was the resigned shrug. But fortunately, the historic preservation of the movement's great masterworks and the publication of scholarship, notably Randell Makinson's Greene & Greene monographs, fueled the current Arts & Crafts revival, and hasn't lost steam since.

The current revival has brought to the fore a new generation of craftspeople to the professions: architects, designers, woodworkers, metal smiths, glass artists, tile makers, textile artisans, and building contractors trained in the restoration of historic buildings. The craftspeople and trades needed for restoring old bungalows and designing new ones are well established, and homeowners have beat paths to their doors. But to what end? The restoration and preservation of the historic homes, of course, must continue. What are the inspirations for new work? Will the revival be a studied re-creation of turn-of-the-century bungalows, or will it result in fresh new house design based on the original principles of bungalow design?

posite) Glass crystal nightstand designed for the Studley residence, with fundamental materials—cast glass, hammered copper, and carved e—expressed in a direct way. Matthew Bialecki, architect.

This magnificent stairway in the Studley house is one of the finest examples of design and craftsmanship in the Arts & Crafts revival.

STYLE

Jill Kessenich, Associate AIA

One of the great things about a bungalow is that it's most often a one-story house, which makes it a viable retirement home.

Jill Kessenich, Associate AIA

Ask anyone in Milwaukee, Wisconsin, what a bungalow is and nine times out of ten, they can simply point to one on their street. It is a clapboard or brick home with a hipped or jerkin-head roof and a three-season front porch. It is a story and a half tall, and the upper level has an open attic, or maybe has one bedroom with a dormer window. As a kid, that attic was a great place to play, but to the designer and builder, it was ready-made for expansion. Milwaukee is just one of many cities that came of age dur-

This contemporary home, designed by Curtis Gelotte Architects, is built in the spirit of Greene & Greene.

Typical bungalow of the mid-1900s from a Boise Payette Lumber Co. plan book.

ing the industrial era, when housing was needed for a growing population and growing families. The bungalow seemed to fit most everyone's requirements.

Most bungalows in America were built in the early 1900s on narrow city lots, grouped in neighborhoods near a local industry. The American bungalow of the mid-1900s typically has a prominent front porch, a low roof pitch, and wide eaves. The narrow end usually faces the street, and the first floor has six rooms, stacked side-by-side: a living room, formal dining room, kitchen on one side, and two bedrooms and a bath on the other side.

The Qualey family home in Santa Monica, vintage 1950s, was remodeled in 1998 to a Greene & Greene–style beauty. This classy new bungalow is complemented with lighting design by Historic Lighting.

Vintage Bungalows: Space

Upon entering a vintage bungalow from the spacious porch, you see there's a built-in bench or boot box in the front hall. You immediately feel the house envelop you with its warmth. Most likely, it's the woodwork, maybe a natural redwood, or Douglas fir, or a richly stained white oak. Even if the woodwork is painted, it's usually abundant, and still gives the rooms a rich quality. The floors will also be wood, maybe a natural maple or vertical-grain fir, but typically oak. In the living room there's almost always a fireplace, and it may be flanked by bookcases and piano windows. It's the perfect place to relax on a chilly evening with a good book and a blazing fire.

In the dining room there will most likely be a built-in china hutch, often with a beveled mirror and, if you're lucky, some stained art glass. This may even have a pass-through to the kitchen. The hutch provides a lot of storage space and doesn't clutter up the room like free-standing furniture can. Maybe there's a window seat, or a bay window that lets in more natural light and gives the room a spacious quality.

The kitchen might still have its original cabinets, which are probably painted white or at least a light color. Perhaps there is a wall-mounted sink or a wood-burning or gas stove. There might even be some funky old linoleum on the floor. Some bungalow kitchens might still have the old icebox and compressor, or at least the cabinet.

The bathroom may have its own set of treasures. If it's in original condition, it will most likely have white hexagonal floor tile, maybe with a colored accent. There could be a tiled wainscot on the walls, or plaster scored to look like tile.

(Left) A small window seat on the second-floor stair landing makes good use of space that would otherwise be relegated to pass-through territory. Courtesy of Historic Lighting.

A spacious entryway in the Maclucas house is warmed by a beautiful collection of Oriental rugs and a gallery of photographs. Courtesy of Historic Lighting.

(upper left) Dark wainscoting sets off the pedestal sink in the Qualey powder room. Courtesy of Historic Lighting.

(Above) Built-in benches in the fireplace nook take less space than freestanding furniture would. Design by David M. Schwarz / Architectural Services Inc.

Juidiith Clawson of Simply Fetched took a Wrightian approach to this stairway design. Mahogany and lacewood below the banister pop the grain. The whole look is artistic, making an attractive transition between the open space of the main floor and the private family area upstairs. Architectural detailing and space planning by Juidiith Clawson of Simply Fetched; Michael and Jane Mangelson, owners.

A pedestal sink and claw-foot tub would be the norm, and the toilet might have a wooden tank mounted high on the wall, or even a round tank. The original shower could have a sunflower-shaped head surrounded by a round or curved curtain rod. The bedrooms will most likely be small and cozy.

One of the great things about a bungalow is that it's most often a one-story house, which makes it a viable retirement home for when negotiating stairs can be a problem. It's also a good first home that can be expanded upstairs as the need arises. Sometimes staircases are narrow and steep, or hidden behind a door. These can often be opened up or reworked to make a more natural transition between first- and second-floor living spaces.

The rich wood from the main floor of the Qualey house continues up the stairway, for a smooth blending of two living areas. This kind of wood detailing is reminiscent of the brothers Greene. Courtesy of Historic Lighting.

A NEIGHBORHOOD HOUSE

In larger terms, vintage bungalows are ideal for today's living because of where they were built. They are most often in first-ring suburbs of major cities, or just blocks from the downtown in smaller towns. That makes them close to shopping, entertainment and other services, often within walking distance.

The trees that were planted when the houses were built are now mature, and provide welcome shade from the summer heat. Their towering canopies give the streetscape an inviting quality.

The houses themselves also provide a neighborly quality. The front porches are a place where children can play, or a parent can watch from a distance. This promotes interaction with neighbors.

Many people living in vintage bungalows are attracted to them for the same reasons: they're affordable, they're close to the city, and the houses are built with character. These homeowners also have something else in common. With the value of these houses on the rise, they all have some ideas for restoring, remodeling, or adding onto their houses. Any improvements they make will add to their equity.

Midcentury bungalow designs usually incorporated porches, where neighborly interchanges were stimulated as people spent time outdoors.

A CHANGING HOUSE

Whether you own a modest kit bungalow or one that was designed by a local architect, chances are that your house has gone through a few changes over the years. The rooms most likely remodeled were the kitchen and the bathroom, as the advent of amenities like refrigerator/freezers and stand-up showers were seen as modern advances, and most people wanted to obtain them. Later on, items such as pre-manufactured cabinets, built-in ovens, and fiberglass shower surrounds began to appear.

Unfortunately, most of these new innovations were not built in styles that complemented the old-fashioned bungalow and, to our eyes, might clash with the original built-ins and furniture. One of the first steps in restoring these spaces to their original charm, while maintaining modern functions, is to identify the style, or styles, of your bungalow. Then, when you plan a larger project such as a major remodeling or addition, you can know what to look for in products and designs.

There are a multitude of bungalow styles around. Yours could be one of several variations. It could very likely have Craftsman detailing on the outside yet be Colonial Revival on the inside. There are some identifying features of the different styles. And since the bungalow is eclectic by nature, styles can be interpreted and applied in various ways.

The more one knows about the history of the bungalow one lives in, the easier it is to make renovations and updates in keeping with the character of the house.

VERNACULAR STYLES

QUEEN ANNE (1890–1905)

Queen Anne cottages or bungalows sprang up on the East Coast and quickly spread to the West as a more simple and economical alternative to the grander Queen Anne two-storied houses.

- Typically clad in clapboards or shingles
- Medium-pitched roof
- Porch with a small amount of gingerbread ornamentation
- Interiors typically Victorian, with wallpapered walls
- A picture molding a foot or two below the ceiling
- Non-typical drawing room/parlor configuration of same-era houses; rooms merged into one living room

CRAFTSMAN (1905–25)

Sometimes called Arts & Crafts, this style is most often associated with the state of California.

- Most prominent element is the low-pitched roof with wide, overhanging eaves
- Triangular gable ends often feature substantial wood brackets, or knee-braces
- Sometimes has massive beams without brackets
- Beams and other structural elements often appear larger than necessary
- Replaces mere decoration with elements that suggest strength and substance
- Often has more than one front-facing gable
- Porch columns always prominent but can be of various styles
- Materials like river rock, cobblestone, and clinker brick incorporated for contrast into piers, chimneys, and retaining walls
- Brick used in a variety of ways, for instance rough-textured style on the chimney exterior, contrasting with a smoother, often glazed, style for the mantel
- Interiors usually of natural or darkly stained wood, e.g., redwood or Douglas fir
- Plaster walls often painted deep natural shades, such as terra-cotta, gold, or green
- Walls might be covered in burlap or grass cloth

California Style

Sometimes this reference is used to describe vernacular variations of what we call Craftsman style.

- A simplified, usually stucco version of the Craftsman or Arts & Crafts style
- Relates indoors to outdoors with large windows, south-facing sun porch, or open courtyard

Airplane

Another variation on the California Craftsman style.

- Distinctive raised second level with four separate side walls rising up in the center of the main roofline, creating a sort of cockpit

Oriental, Japanese, and "Japo-Swiss"

A natural offshoot of the Craftsman style. Many western architects were influenced by Asian architecture, and the bungalow lent itself particularly well because of its structural emphasis. Some versions are subtle, while others are exaggerated and almost cartoon-like.

- Upsweeping gable peaks and pagoda-derived forms

Chicago Style (1920–30)

Chicago style is considered a melding of Craftsman and Prairie School influences.

- Almost always of brick construction
- Built narrow and long for city lots
- Typically steeper-pitched roof, often hipped or jerkin-head
- Often has leaded art-glass windows
- Small three-season porch or sunroom
- Designed and materials selected to accommodate snow loads and colder climates; hence, most popular in the Midwest

PRAIRIE SCHOOL (1900–1920)

This style is heavily associated with Chicago and the work of Frank Lloyd Wright and other architects especially in the area of Oak Park, Illinois.

- Low-pitched, hipped roof and wide eaves
- Horizontal lines and low foundations
- Usually brick or stucco
- Entrances commonly asymmetrical to the center of the house, often hidden from view

REVIVAL STYLES (1890–1940)

These bungalows were starting to be referred to as "cottages" in plan books and other publications, as the popularity of the term bungalow was waning in the 1930s. One plan book company, W. W. Dixon, cleverly created three exterior "cottage" styles for the same bungalow plan.

English Tudor/English Cottage (1890–1930)
Also referred to as British or English Arts & Crafts.

- Rooflines suggest the original thatched roofs of their predecessors
- Typically brick or a combination of brick and stucco
- Half-timbering details
- Casement windows sometimes leaded in a diamond pattern
- A flattened "Tudor arch" might be added to the fireplace

Mission, Spanish Colonial, and Pueblo (1890–1930)
Though not limited to the southern states, most often seen in places with a Spanish past.

- Mission or Mediterranean styles drew on Hispanic church architecture
- Spanish Colonial drew influences from Mexico and Spain
- Pueblo Revival drew on Southwest Native American style
- All similar in their use of stucco walls that resemble adobe bricks
- Clay-tile roofs

- Rounded or stepped arches, often in an arcade
- Simple ornamentation of trellis or pergola outside, fireplace or tile-accented floor inside

Colonial (1910–40)

The end of World War I seemed to spawn an interest in most of these revival styles, Colonial Revival being the most popular.

- Classical details include rounded columns and porch roofs with flat arches
- Entrances are symmetrical with painted white moldings and the occasional dentil
- Clad in either brick (usually red) or narrow clapboard siding
- Simple interiors
- Woodwork usually painted white

SWISS CHALET & LOG CABIN (1900–30)

Both styles are heavily associated with the Arts & Crafts movement and rustic furniture. The log cabin bungalow's popularity is attributed to the rise of rustic lodges and distinctive national park architecture. In the Adirondacks, wealthy weekenders built camps for themselves that resembled Swiss chalets.

- Often have cutout moldings and railings, or those made with rough-hewn branches
- Chalet or chateaux: front-facing gable
- Cabin: side-facing gable with dormer windows

MODERNE (1930–40)

The last early-twentieth-century bungalow style, and the one with the shortest run. Often called Art Deco, now referred to as Streamline Moderne.

- Styling inspired by clean lines of current industrial design, such as Airstream trailers and Frigidaire refrigerators
- Queen Mary-inspired porthole windows and metal trim
- Glass brick and terra-cotta for ornamental accent

TO START?:

Jill Kessenich, Associate AIA

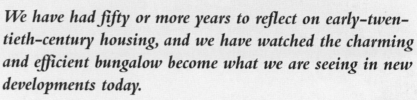

We have had fifty or more years to reflect on early-twentieth-century housing, and we have watched the charming and efficient bungalow become what we are seeing in new developments today.

Jill Kessenich, Associate AIA

Now that you have a good foundation of the history and distinctive styles of the bungalow, you can actually start to prioritize the work that you want to do on your bungalow. Most successful renovation projects are the result of careful planning. Even if the project is to be completed in stages, a master plan that coordinates current and future activities will ensure a smooth transition from one project to another. Architects or other design professionals can help to develop the "big picture" as well as provide valuable insight into the possibilities for your bungalow.

Antique tin ceiling tiles make a classy backsplash for a period sink and stove. Everything about this kitchen is reminiscent of the 1940s bungalow, right down to the tablecloth.

Before starting any major remodeling project, it is a good idea to update any systems that are worn out or even dangerous. Most vintage bungalows are at least sixty years old and some are more than a hundred. The oldest ones were the first houses to have indoor plumbing. In these older bungalows, electricity was still in its infancy and often accompanied coal gas lighting. Central heating systems consisted of large inefficient wood or coal-fired boilers and furnaces. Home inspectors and professional electricians and plumbers can help you to evaluate the condition of your current mechanical systems and assess the impact that future renovations will have on them. Although this can be the least-glamorous and rewarding work you do on your house, updating these mechanical systems serves as the foundation for much of the work to follow. Here are some things you should address.

• Will your electrical system handle all the appliances, lighting, and other amenities you want to incorporate into your remodel? Fuse boxes and three or four circuits of knob-and-tube wiring (wax- and cloth-wrapped wires with porcelain insulators and sleeves) were standard in most bungalows. Upgrading with modern circuit breakers and properly sized and grounded wiring networks will help safeguard against an electrical fire and will make future modifications easy and safe.

• The plumbing systems in many bungalows are in need of upgrading. Most cast-iron drain systems continue to work well and have some advantages over plastic piping, particularly sound transmission and inadvertent perforation. Their disadvantage lies in the difficulty of attaching additional drains and possible leaks around connections. Water-supply piping is often in need of replacement for a variety of health and safety reasons. Iron or steel pipes corrode from

Built-in cabinets, cupboards, and shelves are classic elements of bungalow style. They allow for personal expression by providing space for collectibles such as the lamps, animals, and helicopter fleet that brighten the perimeters of this room.

the inside, gradually constricting or closing off the pipe. This decreases water pressure, adds impurities to the water, and can produce an occasional leak. Some supply pipes in older houses and neighborhoods are made of lead that leaches into the water. Replacement with copper or plastic tubing and the proper solders and connections will provide a long-lived and safe water supply.

Two panels of three-over-one windows meeting in the corner of the room take advantage of the sun through most of the day, providing heat in winter and letting in plenty of light under the overhanging eaves. Designed and interiors by Highland Group.

•Most bungalows had some type of solid fuel (wood or coal) heat, relying on natural convection currents to distribute it around the house. This system, while quiet, heated only a short distance from the source and required oversized ducts and pipes to overcome friction. The development of fan or pump-assisted, high-efficiency, gas-fired furnaces and boilers distributed heat evenly throughout the house. A giant steel "octopus" furnace in the basement can be replaced by a suitcase-sized model and vented directly through the foundation wall with PVC tubing. Other advantages of this upgrade range from lower heating bills to an increase in useable space through the removal of the furnace and utility chimney.

• A renovation project may also be a good time to add insulation or replace windows. Depending on the climate in your area and the price of fuel, these improvements may or may not make economic sense. Local weatherization specialists can advise you in this matter. Attic insulation is generally easy to do and almost always makes sense. Wall insulation is much more difficult and will require removing at least some of the siding to drill holes in the sheathing and blow in the insulation. The siding is then replaced. Some contractors will drill through the siding and patch the hole with a plug. As you can imagine, this technique is a visual compromise, and insulation done by this method is spotty at best, as it tends to get hung up on wires, pipes, and blocking within the wall and may not be worth the effort.

• Windows may be upgraded with storm windows or replacement sashes with insulated glass. Often a large part of the character of a bungalow is derived from its windows. Muntin or leaded patterns are difficult and expensive to replicate, so careful attention should be paid to the construction and proportions of the replacement components to maintain the original character.

Many fine books have been devoted to bungalow restoration. After some serious homework, a restorer can decide what kind of restoration or renovation is feasible for their budget and appropriate for their lifestyle.

Living rooms and dining rooms are usually the easiest to restore since they are the most likely to be in original condition, as the way we use them today

This restored living room is trimmed out in the Arts & Crafts style, including dark wood trim, a high-back craftsman-style settee, and plentiful period-look lighting.

A small pantry off the kitchen helps keep some of the
clutter out of view. The refrigerator as well as dishes
and foodstuff can be hidden behind a closed door but
are easily accessible. Bead board is used for both the
wainscoting and the cabinet fronts below.

isn't all that different from the way they were used eighty or ninety years ago. If they have been modified, the changes were usually cosmetic; carpeting and inappropriate wallpaper are pretty easy to tear out.

However, because we have changed the way we use kitchens and bathrooms, these are most likely the rooms that have been remodeled. Originally built to be very utilitarian, and with one user, these rooms have become an extension of the recreational parts of our houses and lives. Entertaining today often involves both partners cooking dinner for friends or family, who are often looking on from a family room or eating area.

Even the bathroom has become a place for relaxation, with whirlpool tubs, steam showers, and spas. These luxury items

This classic California bungalow with airplane roof was home to Tom Mix, cowboy hero of the silver screen.

might even be desired in a home gym, which could include a current pool or full-size hot tub. On a more practical note, bathrooms have grown bigger, with more than one sink and other fixtures to accommodate two working adults.

Most of the original bungalows never anticipated a need for these extra spaces, so their original footprints (the shape on the lot) often don't accommodate them. If you are one of the lucky bungalow owners who still have an unfinished attic, an extra bathroom or master suite may be able to fit into that sort of space. But for first-floor additions, building back is usually your best bet, since that is usually where most of the buildable room is on your lot.

Add a Space

• One common design problem is expanding the kitchen and possibly creating an adjacent room. This might be a simple nook for eating breakfast, a larger sunroom, or a full-size family room. Kitchen expansions often involve enlarging the work triangle (sink, range, and refrigerator) to accommodate another cook, a worktable, or island. Larger or additional appliances may also be the reason for expansion; there weren't dishwashers or refrigerator/freezers in the early bungalows. Maybe a walk-in pantry can be dismantled, creating more room for appliances and cabinets or an eating area with a view into the backyard.

• Another common desire is to create a home office or designated workspace. This could be as simple as working a desk or computer area into the kitchen-cabinet layout, or it may require devoting an entire room to a private office. Sometimes a small bedroom can be converted, but it may require an addition.

• Expanding out the side of the house is often difficult, as local zoning codes restrict owners to minimum side yard setbacks (the distance from the house to the lot line). Even adding a dormer can be difficult. Until recently in some cities, second-story dormers were only built with a variance, as they infringed on the "light and air" rights of neighbors. Perhaps at one time this law was necessary to control overcrowding of neighborhoods, but now it discourages inner-city property improvements. These laws are slowly being modified to accommodate and encourage people to improve existing city properties rather than force them to build yet another suburban home.

If you live in a city that allows this kind of expansion, adding a dormer or two is often a great solution. It doesn't change the size of the footprint of the house, so no additional foundation work is required. It simply allows for useable headroom where there was only floor space. Many larger dormer additions house master bedroom suites or additional bedrooms, while smaller ones can contain bathrooms or a little nook for reading or a desk.

An L-shaped addition is one way to add space. The private outdoor nook created by the L is a side benefit.

Adding a dormer or two is a great solution for growth because no foundation work is required. It simply adds headroom where there was only floor space before.

The Bungalow Revived

We have had fifty or more years to reflect on early-twentieth-century housing, and we have watched the charming and efficient bungalow become what we are seeing in new developments today. We cherish our cozy bungalows, on tree-lined streets within walking distance of a little business district in our favorite city. We love their quirky charms: built-in benches or china hutches; clothes chutes or pass-throughs.

If you own a bungalow, you are probably aware that the style is in a revival, as can be seen in magazines like *American Bungalow* and *Old House Journal* and a number of books on their history and restoration. You might also have begun to notice that a few new bungalows are cropping up here and there, designed by people who have long respected the original ones and don't feel the need to reinvent the wheel.

The stage is set for a revival of bungalow neighborhoods that can equal the manageability and charm of earlier decades.

: THE NEW BUNGALOW :

REVIVAL

by Christian Gladu

The site, the craftsmanship, the materials, and the design executed correctly will equal a sum much greater than its parts—we call it the bungalow.

Christian Gladu, The Bungalow Company

With its emphasis on handcrafted beauty, quality workmanship, and respect for natural materials, today's bungalow style offers friendly streetscapes and sensible, ecologically oriented homes that nurture twenty-first-century families.

Most homes built today contain space that is poorly utilized, consume far more energy than is reasonable, and are often built from inferior materials that just don't stand the

New bungalows, like this one built by The Bungalow Company, integrate the style and timeless charm of the past with a modern point of view.

test of time. As we move from the industrial age to the information age, the bungalow revival is a natural transition. The bungalow stands strong as an icon of simpler times and is responding to the increasing complexity of land development and the harsh reality of urban sprawl. New urbanism and other planning concepts have provided more homes in less space while at the same time developing more community-oriented neighborhoods. This development style also results in less commuting and the preservation of our undeveloped lands. As we return to traditionally planned neighborhoods, we recognize the bungalow as a philosophy first and a building style second. As such, it offers the following:

- A proactive approach to community through design.

- A tool to transition our culture to a simpler way of life.

- A future that embraces environmental challenges.

For the Jacobs residence in Pasadena, architect Gilbert Lee Hershberger created a friendly streetscape that blends the house with the yard.

Planning

Densely planned neighbor-
hoods, if properly designed
and executed, evolve into
thriving communities for
generations to enjoy.

*In the best bungalow
neighborhoods, such as
this one designed by The
Bungalow Company, all
facades of the house are
designed with the atten-
tion to detail as if they
faced the street.*

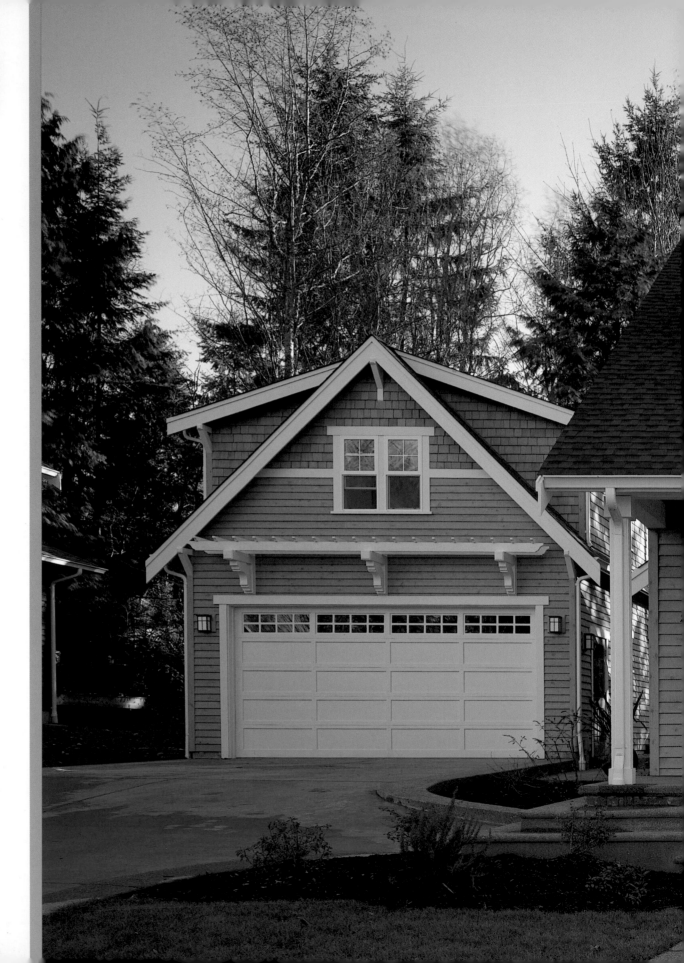

SQUARE FOOTAGE

Since the 1920s, the average family has decreased in size, while the square footage of the average home has doubled, increasing the amount of space that is poorly utilized. The new bungalow is modest in size by today's standards, and includes floor plans that are designed for a more casual lifestyle—floor plans that are more open and informal than their predecessors.

Determining a house's value by the square foot is similar to buying an automobile by the pound. Ironically, smaller older homes in established neighborhoods bring a premium cost per square foot, supporting the theory that bigger is not necessarily better and that homebuyers are willing to pay for design and neighborhood character. The challenge in traditionally planned neighborhoods is to encourage the building, real estate, and banking communities to divorce themselves from their preconceptions of how to value homes and realize that square footage is not always the be-all and end-all of building. The truer concept is how that square footage is utilized.

The temptation to build larger is twofold: first, the larger home will typically cost less per square foot and, secondly, for builders, more square footage typically elevates the asking price. The downsides to this are both visual and environmental. Visually, the more space a home requires, the less opportunity there is to develop outdoor spaces. This also makes it hard to maintain a comfortable level of personal and private spaces.

Environmentally, bungalows not only use space wisely, but they also take advantage of the common natural materials indigenous to their particular area of the country.

These plans by The Bungalow Company are modest in size by today's standards but more open and informal than their predecessors.

NORTH TOWN

North Town Woods is a community neighborhood of crafts-man-style bungalows on Bainbridge Island, Washington. It is centrally located near schools, shopping, and public trans-portation. It is a revival of simple, well-crafted designs from the past, a community with a look that recalls a bygone era. Designed by The Bungalow Company, built by Reese Construction, and developed by Madison Avenue Develop-ment, these bungalow-style homes feature traditional crafts-manship and design. Careful attention to historic details from tile fireplaces to period lighting gives these homes a truly authentic style. They blend modern amenities with nostalgic themes, providing the best of both worlds.

NEIGHBORHOODS

Traditionally planned neighborhoods are most successful when they are located within walking distance of schools, work, parks, transportation hubs, and shopping. Basic real estate economics would suggest that bungalow properties should be more expensive than land thirty miles from town without local amenities. Building denser communities in these urban areas gives the inhabitants the ability to reduce their reliance on the automobile. However, in dense neighborhoods, the ability to build expansively is limited by the actual size of the lot. Bungalows in new neighborhoods should be built to last in order to have the community appreciate in both actual dollar value as well as social desirability. Consistency in design and detailing is always important but is imperative when designing for a neighborhood; views are often territorial. To create visual value and character, all elevations of a home must be designed as if they were the front door. The pursuit of desirable neighborhoods and communities is a collective effort and requires cooperation of all parties, including neighborly etiquette in co-developing beautiful homes with a true sense of place.

Bungalows in new neighborhoods should be built to last a hundred years or more. This requires attention to selection of materials, as well as heating and cooling systems and fixtures.

Merging Yesterday With Today

The goal of new bungalows is to synthesize original exterior design and details while adapting the interior plans to reflect lifestyles of today—essentially, to take off from where the first builders and designers of the American bungalows left off, and bring these homes and communities to the next level by meeting the needs of today's families. Designing the new bungalow is truly a cooperative effort, shared by the designers, craftsmen, and clients.

Designing the new bungalow transcends individual designs and requires one to look closely at the renaissance that is redefining our culture: Families are rediscovering their past and are searching for nostalgic connections to unite them with their history and their modern community. They are also looking to create a comfortable, functional home. The following are basic elements that help capture the bungalow spirit and meet the needs of today's homeowners.

Designing the new bungalow is truly a cooperative effort, shared by the designers, craftsmen, interior designers, and clients. Here a contemporary paint technique by Lisa Lacaden and Mary Jane Papazian complements traditional craftsmanship.

PORCHES

The bungalow porch serves as a visual break from the street, softening the contrast between street, landscape, and architecture. It draws from agrarian life and reinforces a connection with nature and community. The porch and front entry also serve as a physical portal from public space to the privacy of the home, including setting the stage for the interior with details and scale.

NOOKS

Bungalow designs have always been synonymous with traditional living space augmented by intimate spaces with specific uses. The use of inglenooks and breakfast nooks give the home extra space without over-scaling the floor plan. These spaces also provide opportunities to use quality materials with more detail to create memorable spaces. When using intimate spaces, homeowners are often more aware of the details, and the use of superior materials drives the experience home. These elements often create visual breaks in or between rooms.

The bungalow porch serves as a physical portal from public space to the privacy of the home, including setting the stage for the interior details and scale.

NATURAL LIGHT

One of the key factors is to develop spaces with natural light from two or more directions while being sensitive to the views and privacy that are created. An example would be the use of high windows flanking a fireplace or the use of decorative art glass to obscure entry doors or bathroom views.

DEFINING SPACE

Defining space without overuse of walls is what makes the bungalow "live big." Delineating areas with dropped and cased doorways or archways sends a clear message to inhabitants that they are changing spaces. Framed doorways are opportunities to direct views to other areas and give focus to outdoor scenes. The focusing of views gives the bungalow the ability to bring the outside in and the inside out, reinforcing our connection with nature. There is also great opportunity to create changes in color, material, and details.

In the Michael and Jane Mangelson house, designer Juidiith Clawson designed a quiet receiving area just off the front entrance. The formal dining area shares space with a sitting room, separated not by doors but simply by an arch with pillars on either end. This area of the home has a formal look without being ostentatious.

KITCHENS

Today's bungalow kitchens have been transformed from isolated work centers to the heart of the home. Kitchens offer plentiful workspaces while serving as hubs for the home. They are also areas to express crafts-man detailing and work-manship. Additionally, the more centrally featured kitchen has brought the ability to introduce more natural light into the home.

Stainless-steel finishes of industrial-grade ranges and refrigerators are a good fit. Other items like apron sinks and wall-mounted faucets give newly done spaces vintage charm. Courtesy Ashmore/Kessenich.

Custom cabinetry designs by Juidiith Clawson are based on craftsman but with an edgy look. Under-cabinet windows bring light and openness to an area that is usually ignored.

New bungalows have answered today's call for master bed-room suites. This room, tastefully painted in period style by Lisa Lacaden and Mary Jane Papazian, creates a private retreat that is an antidote for a hectic schedule.

Multipaned windows with broad casing act almost like a work of art on this bedroom wall. Paint colors were selected to maintain peacefulness in this master suite. Design by Juidiith Clawson of Simply Fetched.

MASTER BEDROOMS

New bungalows have adjusted to the trends of master bedrooms by applying the principles of creating private retreats that serve as an antidote to hectic schedules. As such, the bedrooms are designed with large attached baths and ample closet space. The goal is to make rooms that reflect their owners' lifestyles.

Incorporating some "today" elements in an Arts & Crafts design, Juidiith Clawson of Simply Fetched created a bath alcove in the master suite that is as beautiful as it is functional. A rustic cedar liner bears a tree motif modeled on a Frank Lloyd Wright Oak Park design. Michael and Jane Mangelson house.

Classic bathroom elements such as pedestal sinks, honeycomb tile, and wainscoting make this bathroom clean and spacious. Courtesy Ashmore/Kessenich.

BATHROOMS

Simply put, new bungalows incorporate more bathrooms into their floor plans than were there traditionally.

Bathrooms are also utilitarian in their use of space and components. They are designed with classic elements such as pedestal sinks, built-in medicine cabinets, and careful details in tile work and trim but also incorporate some of today's luxuries, such as larger tubs.

WORKSPACES

Work-at-home spaces have transitioned well into the bungalow, but they do not need to be expansive. It is more important that they are properly located to either provide adequate privacy for concentration or to be more public for facilitating interaction among family members. Many of the more traditional spaces can actually double quite effectively as work and living spaces. Example: a breakfast nook

At-home workspaces do not have to be expansive to work well. This design by John Malick integrates the workspace into the kitchen area, creating a unique family hub.

A home office at the front of the house overlooks the goings-on in the neighborhood. Juidiith Clawson designed the space to be multifunctional. Built-ins (the desk with drawers, and book cases lining the wall behind (unseen) make this room comfy for reading or working. Dark bronze roller screens at the windows allow maximum light with minimum intrusion. Another nice feature is a restored tin ceiling (unseen). The same tin was used on the ceiling and as wainscoting in the guest bathroom.

with an Internet connection serves not only as a place of communication, but may also support household, family, and financial record keeping. It may also provide an area for parental guidance of children using the Internet or completing homework assignments while still allowing for meal preparation.

The proper detailing for climate and the correct heating, cooling, and ventilation are the backbone of building longevity. Conservation is a holistic approach: build smaller, more energy-efficient homes on less land and in locations that will reduce the amount of miles driven per year. All homes shown are by The Bungalow Company.

Building footprints dimensioned in modules of four-foot increments is a smart way to save on materials in the framing stages, according to Ashmore/Kessenich Design. All homes shown here are from their plan book.

How to Get "the Look" in New Construction

Jim McCord, AIA

Let's assume for a moment that you wanted to recapture a part of the Arts & Crafts philosophy and introduce some level of calmness, beauty, and simplicity into your lifestyle. Or perhaps you are one of those individuals who is seeking a cozy abode that better expresses the way you live. No matter what you might be looking for—whether it is an Arts & Crafts–style lamp or a new bungalow-style home filled with interior enhancements such as wood trim, copper and iron hardware, period-looking light fixtures, stenciled draperies, and a full contingent of new craftsman furniture—the Gustav Stickleys, Elbert Hubbards, and Sears of the new century offer plenty of choices. (See Resources.)

It is appropriate that today's market offers various levels of quality, design, and fabrication. As such, individuals of all economic levels are able to enjoy the Arts & Crafts lifestyle to the degree they feel is appropriate.

Interior enhancements such as this copper lamp, windows, and furniture are being created by today's Stickleys and Hubbards. All of the accessories seen here were made by the homeowner, Audel Davis.

Once you have decided you want to live in a home styled like a new bungalow, one of the first things you need to decide is what kind of home you are seeking. Do you want a small urban, single-family home on a small lot, or a more spacious suburban-type home with a significant yard and square footage to match? Or do you want to buy your dream site and select a plan from one of the designers capable of providing bungalow plans reminiscent of the period but interpreted to meet the needs of contemporary living? Another option is to acquire land and hire an architect to custom design your new bungalow within the parameters you define and the level of detail and period harmony that you feel is appropriate.

This John Malick interior was custom-designed to fit the parameters of the owners' desire for detail and period harmony. Plentiful natural light and ample artificial lighting make this room comfortable at all times of the day. Note how the area rug delineates the use of space in an open setting.

CHOOSING A DEVELOPER

Because "bungalow" can be defined in a number of different ways, developers who specialize in new bungalow houses come from different experiences and mind-sets. Some are sensitive to the bungalow style as a representation of a historic building type and carry their commitment to the style as far as possible within the scope of the residential development as the sales price allows. Others simply reflect the bungalow style as an exterior architectural expression and leave the interior to the devices of the new owner. Making the most of your bungalow before you close escrow will diminish the scope of work required to make your house a home once you take occupancy.

For this location in the Colorado Rockies, David M. Schwarz / Architectural Services Inc. designed the house to suit a mountain landscape. Its orientation takes optimal advantage of both sun and shade.

(Below) Highland Group designed this exterior using natural materials consistent with its locale near the mountains. Soffits, fascias, and exposed rafters maintain the authenticity of craftsman styling.

THE WELL-DESIGNED BUNGALOW

The well-designed bungalow respects the land on which it is built by optimizing sun orientation or shade as best suits the climatic requirements, considering prevailing winds, and providing protection or cooling as needed. The building is formed from materials that are consistent with its locale, such as natural stone, common wood species, or clay bricks. These make a harmonious transition to the land, both physically and visually, capturing the feeling of comfort and harmony that are the hallmarks of the bungalow style.

UPGRADES

Following is an overview of some relatively simple choices you can make to enhance a new bungalow-style home built on speculation. It is possible to extrapolate some of these methods as topics of discussion for use when sitting down with a designer or an architect to plan your new bungalow. These suggestions just scratch the surface of considerations that

should be taken into account when doing a significant remodeling or engaging in construction of a new bungalow. This information, coupled with review of the products and services itemized in the Resources, will enable you to begin your mission toward ownership of a new bungalow with a clear frame of reference and initial direction.

Wood Trim

If you buy a home during the initial framing process, you may have an opportunity to add some upgrades or more-appropriate interior finish selections prior to completion of the home. One upgrade, installing simple rectilinear stain-grade wood trim at doors, windows, and other openings can be handled with a materials and finish-up charge without significant additional labor. Many times, the simplicity of the detail fabrication of Arts & Crafts–inspired wood trim eliminates some of the mitered corners and detailed coping transitions that exist in many new homes today. The change in the look and feel is significant.

Light fixtures such as this one from Historic Lighting can be chosen to enhance the Arts & Crafts feel of a conventionally constructed home.

Ashmore/Kessenich upgraded this design to include an atmospheric fireplace with a tile fireplace surround. The built-in bookcases on either side are enviable.

No element can change the character of a home more dramatically than paint. This ceiling (opposite and above) was detailed by Lisa Lacaden and Mary Jane Papazian to complement the reproduction light fixtures and built-in cabinetry.

The designer-painted surface makes a classy background for this simple wall arrangement. Courtesy of Historic Lighting.

Paint

No inexpensive element can change the character of a home more dramatically than paint. Since it needs to be painted anyway, making the right color selections can be an important part in realizing your vision. Fortunately, a few paint manufacturers offer their versions of historic colors. Sherwin Williams's Preservation Palette is recommended: they call their colors by names such as Bungalow Blue, Studio Blue Green, Roycrofters Arts & Crafts colors, etcetera. Some manufacturers offer preselected combinations of colors for body, window sash, and trim. Interior colors, as well as exterior colors, can be harmonized by using these period palettes.

If you want help selecting colors, you may want to engage a design service that specializes in historic restorations. A few resources pop up on the Internet when you search the key words "historic paint colors."

Caution: When it comes to period colors, subtle variations can sometimes result in disaster. Color selections should be made from period color renditions and oftentimes "close" is not good enough.

Walnut trim on this oak flooring adds definition to the simplistic design of this living room. The decor is a personalized melding of contemporary with Arts & Crafts. Courtesy of Historic Lighting.

Floor Coverings

Floor coverings can be handled in much the same manner. Whether using carpet, ceramic tile, or wood, make choices that reflect the bungalow style. Often a selection can be made within the products that the contractor would normally use that would better suit the Arts & Crafts palette. Ask yourself what material suits the other features of the house.

This high-end home designed by architect Gilbert Lee Hershberger displays a richness of craftsmanship associated with the original Arts & Crafts movement.

The most common floor materials that mimic the style are softwoods (pine or fir), hardwoods, and vinyl or linoleum. Softwoods that are put together using a tongue-and-groove method are quite costly today—consider the savings you may have accrued in other areas and if it is still affordable, this would be a great place to splurge. If it is not feasible, oak or maple flooring is an equally wonderful, but less-expensive, alternative.

If linoleum is preferred, look for companies that offer some vintage-looking patterns that would complement the Arts & Crafts look you are trying to achieve.

Kitchens and Bathrooms

Due to the changes in technology and needs (for instance, we now like spas and big open kitchens that weren't part of the original bungalow movement), these rooms are difficult to design in a manner absolutely consistent with an original bungalow, but plumbing and hardware manufacturers are offering some period-style fixtures that are appropriate for early or late bungalow styles. Pedestal sinks and tubs, claw-foot tubs, period faucets, pull-chain toilets—all these can bring

The twentieth century meets the twenty-first: stainless-steel appliances fit right in with clean lines of the cabinetry in this home. Both photos courtesy of Historic Lighting.

bungalow charm into your new house or into your remodeled rooms. Brand-name items are available at big-box outlets and could be traded for the standard plumbing fixtures that were destined for your house, and some pricier versions are available through the trade. Your contractor should be able to purchase from any of these exclusive sources.

There are excellent references for original period kitchens and bathrooms, two of which are *Bungalow Kitchens* and *Bungalow Bathrooms,* both by Jane Powell and photographed by Linda Svendsen. The examples pictured in these books are of vintage and remodeled homes, and there are both period-true examples and compromise interpretations. Studying these books will surely help you decide what you want your rooms to look like.

"Contemporary materials give this Arts & Crafts look a contemporary edge," says interior designer Valerie Paoli-Johnson. Slate lines the tub surround and covers the floor. Custom cabinetry throughout the house, in cherry and oak, evokes a period feeling as well. Plumbing and hardware manufacturers offer fixtures appropriate for early or late bungalow styles, such as these from Kohler. Design by Highland Group.

Fixtures from Historic Lighting complement the Greene and Greene-style cabinetry and tile flooring.

Historic Lighting brings period-style lighting into the twenty-first century in this craftsman-inspired bathroom.

Hardware

A variety of hardware styles can be appropriate for your new bungalow, based upon fabrication type and materials. Hammered black iron, hammered copper, and wooden knobs matching the species of the wood in the cabinet when stained, are common accessory finishes of the period that are still available today. This hardware is available in all price ranges, the most expensive being that which faithfully reproduces the period. There are a variety of lesser-cost hardware choices that provide the look without the price, such as bin pulls made famous on the Hoosier cabinets of the period. In black iron, brushed nickel, unlacquered brass, or possibly chrome, they add a period touch to a kitchen, especially if painted-wood cabinet surfaces are used. Nickel or chrome in the kitchen can provide a link with range trim, plumbing, and other typical kitchen finishes.

Door hardware can go through a similar metamorphosis. Bungalow doors were generally equipped with hardware that was an alternative to the bright brass of Victorian homes. Antique brass that is currently available is much like bright brass in that it acquires an uneven tarnish through normal use in a manner that is inconsistent with the durable type of finishes adopted by the bungalow style.

Although the general layout of a traditional bungalow kitchen is vastly different from contemporary layouts, care can be taken in the selection of cabinets and appliances to diminish the level of contrast. John Malick, architect.

Finishes should be oil-rubbed bronze (either base metal or over steel) and black iron. These two finishes are standard with many manufacturers and can be acquired with a slight up-charge, again looking at the installation cost as being identical with the hardware sets that the general contractor originally had in mind. These finishes are consistent with the patinated copper, black iron, and other metal tones of Arts & Crafts interiors, and blend better with stained door finishes than do bright brass fixtures.

Bin pulls, made famous by the Hoosier cabinets of the period, are lesser-cost hardware choices that provide the look without the price. Photo courtesy of Historic Lighting.

The tone of this home is established at the front door with an entry hardware set by Hugh Culley and a Pewabic tile inset above. Inside, a stained-glass lamp and ceiling lanterns by Bob Baird extend a warm welcome in the Arts & Crafts style. Design by Highland Group.

When building a new bungalow, make sure that the contractor installs cabinets in period style. These are in the Shaker style, and match the woodwork used on the ceiling and walls. John Malick, architect.

Cabinetry

Take a close look at the kitchen and bathroom cabinetry. Although the general layout of a traditional bungalow kitchen is vastly different from contemporary layouts, care can be taken in the selection of cabinets and appliances to diminish the level of contrast between your new kitchen and that of the period. Try to keep the cabinet layout as basic as possible and augment it with kitchen furniture, if that option is available to you. For instance, if a kitchen plan has an island counter or a peninsula that does not include an appliance or sink, see if the built-in can be deleted and replaced with a piece of furniture such as a butcher block, enamel-top table, or cabinet. Hoosier cabinets and kitchen dressers are appropriate furnishing pieces. Should you be able to eliminate a section of kitchen counter and replace it with one of these fine storage units, you would make a significant change in the look of your kitchen without sacrificing function. There should be a credit involved in removing some of the cabinetry if the changes do not involve a lot of electrical and plumbing reconfiguration.

One step you can take, in general, is making sure that the contractor installs cabinets in the style of this period. Many cabinet manufacturers offer mission- or Shaker-style cabinets. In general, these cabinets, whether they are painted or stained, have a single, flat-panel door framed with rectangular wood and top and bottom rails. The space between the panel and the frame elements is usually either an inside square corner or contains

Mangelson house cabinet detail. Throughout the house, cabinets were designed by Juidiith Clawson using an artistic mix of alderwood and Honduras mahogany with an inlay of ebony and bird's-eye maple. To subdue the wood colors and tie them together, Clawson developed a green wash to paint over all of the cabinet surfaces.

(Above) The divided-pane motif is a classic element of Arts & Crafts style. Marshall Compton chose to accent these panes with a color darker than the surrounding wood.

Glass doors on built-in cabinetry—the craftsman answer to hutches—is a boon for displaying collectibles or vintage dishes. Su Bacon, designer.

(Facing) This built-in unit designed by David M. Schwarz / Architectural Services Inc. combines spaces for both storage and display. The clean look says "quality" all the way.

simple molding, such as quarter-round or an ovoid sticking variety. These doors are fairly straightforward and are consistent with the cabinetry styles of built-in casework of the period, as well as much of the kitchen furniture produced. Selecting one of these alternative patterns usually results in a minimal extra cost and the effect is worth it.

Countertops, Sinks, and Walls

Ceramic tile was one of the most common bungalow materials, followed by wood and galvanized steel. These materials are readily available today, though they cost considerably more than standard-issue Formica coverings.

Most early sinks were white enameled cast-iron units, many of which had a drain board built into one side. There are kitchen sinks today made with ceramic fronts and splashes to emulate these earlier periods. Or if you

A farmhouse-style sink gives a period look to a contemporary kitchen.

Craftsman-style cabinets topped with concrete countertops mix old and new design to create a classic contemporary look. Lighting design by Historic Lighting.

Ceramic tile was one of the most common bungalow
materials that is readily available today.
(Above) Photo courtesy David Papazian.
(Right) Photo courtesy Marshall Compton.

want to spare the expense, a simple white rectangular one- or two-compartment sink should do the trick.

Kitchen walls and countertop backsplashes were often carried out in ceramic tile, which is often beyond the scope of work in new residential construction. The incorporation of the tile accents brings the bungalow spirit into your home.

White plumbing fixtures will fit the bill, but keep an eye out for new models in the old colors. Accents were chrome or nickel and plumbing fixtures and fittings were either oxidized brass (uncoated and shiny for only the first few months) or polished nickel or chrome, which is readily available in the marketplace today.

A Jack and Jill bathroom connecting two children's rooms features a twig mirror in the Adirondack style by Troy Poulson of Millcreek Furniture. Photo courtesy of Highland Group.

Borrowing a touch from the tradition of Gustav Stickley, encouraging words remind those entering the master suite that this is a place to slow down and enjoy the comfort of a safe haven. The door is of vertical-grain fir. Design by Highland Group.

One way to upgrade a spec house is to choose a bungalow-style door. This one is on a Bungalow Company house.

Stained-glass art , designed by Juidiith Clawson for the Mangelson house and executed by Sandy of Excell, is in the Arts & Crafts tradition but is clearly contemporary. Throughout the house, transom windows atop all the doors (unseen) bear sand-blasted glass.

Doors

For early period homes, five-flat-panel doors, single-flat-panel doors, and many other upgrade styles are available for painting or staining at a variety of quality levels. Early involvement in spec houses may afford the owner opportunity to select doors—even if they are factory-hung mass-market units— that can create a level of quality and warmth consistent with the bungalow image. The additional cost then lies in the quality of the materials used by way of a markup in the value of the door unit rather than in additional installation or finish charges.

The dining room and adjacent kitchen in this home designed by Baylis Architects of Bellevue, Washington, open onto a great room. The dining room features a built-in cherry buffet with slate backsplashes; the slate's natural edges echo the mountains of the Pacific Northwest. A dining table and chairs manufactured by Stickley are in a more contemporary crafts-man style. Seen beyond the doorway is a water wall in the home's entry. Photo courtesy Baylis Architect

Lighting

It is possible to buy various versions of a period lamp, obviously with vast differences in materials and fabrication techniques, that vary in price from under $100 to $15,000.

Interior and exterior light fixtures, including ceiling-hung and bracket types, are readily available in today's market. Most broad-market light fixture manufacturers offer some mission-style or Arts & Crafts–style lighting lines. As with all styles of light fixtures, the quality of design as well as materials and methods of manufacture vary greatly. If well selected, light fixtures can last a lifetime. Finish choices are limited on lower-cost lamps, but flat black, oxidized brass, and patinated brass are generally available. Higher-quality

A built-in bench at the bottom of the stairway, gives the entry an inglenook feeling. The stair railing is cherry wood; the floor is Brazilian cherry. Design by Highland Group.

fixtures are typically of heavier gauge, equipped with porcelain sockets consistent with earlier fixtures, and offered in finishes that can handle the level of intended use. For example, oxidized copper fixtures tend to continue to age quite nicely outdoors and do not rust or otherwise degrade over the years. If some natural patination is desired, natural brass fixtures can be ordered unlacquered. The installer should wear soft gloves so that the natural patination evolves over the years to create a rich, honest, mottled antique finish that no manufacturing process can replicate.

If well selected, light fixtures can last a lifetime. John Malick, Hoelter residence.

Embracing the contemporary craftsman, this light fixture by Sam Mossaedi honors those of Greene & Greene. Lighting design by Historic Lighting.

Su Bacon, Historic Lighting

A contemporary lantern by Arroyo Craftsman combines with the rocks and brick to create a warm front porch welcome. Courtesy Historic Lighting.

When looking at the revival of Arts & Crafts lighting, it is important to understand what the original craftsmen were trying to accomplish with their art. Their focus was to reach back to nature and hand craftsmanship. Working with the available technology and using copper, bronze, mica, hand-blown glass, pottery, and wood, their creations were born. The work of Gustav Stickley, Dirk Van Erp, and Roycroft came alive with the use of hammered copper and mica. To create their beautiful lamps, Lewis C. Tiffany, Frank Lloyd Wright, and Charles and Henry Greene used glass to bring nature's landscape inside. The scenic panels and lamps set the tone for the main structure, and the wood artistry of Greene & Greene added one more of nature's elements to the lights.

As it did at the turn of the twentieth century, lighting plays an important design role in today's revival. However, lighting is not meant to stand alone but rather to blend with colors, textures, furnishings, and art to set the mood and accentuate the architecture. It is also designed as to not take away from a setting but to complete the picture, just as one would experience nature.

Sam Mossaedi takes his inspiration from the Gamble House living room lanterns in his mahogany and art glass light fixture. Courtesy Historic Lighting.

As the old saying goes, "times have changed" and so have our lifestyles. Formal living and dining rooms have almost become extinct, replaced by family rooms that are structured to be adjacent to the kitchen areas, which have evolved into being part of the social gathering. This is where lighting becomes critical, because the room is not only a work area but also a space to socialize and relax.

Bedrooms have now become suites, with sitting rooms and personal libraries. Master bathrooms are mini spas, with fireplaces, Jacuzzi tubs, shower and steam combinations and two sinks. Powder rooms have become small galleries where art can be displayed.

Libraries have turned into in-home offices with computers, entertainment centers with stereo and sound systems and video/DVD players, multiple telephone lines, and intercoms.

Family entertaining has also moved outdoors, with decks, pools, barbecues and cooking areas, along with outdoor fireplaces. All of this necessitates the addition of unique and tasteful lighting that reflects the style of the home.

With all of this change comes a diversification of lighting needs. By working with what is available today and remembering that form follows function, it is possible to bring rooms together with light. Whether using originals or reproductions, there are still some traditional design concepts that can be incorporated in today's new bungalows.

(Above) Lighting should blend with colors, textures, furnishings, and art to set the mood and accentuate the architecture. David M. Schwarz / Architectural Services Inc.

Working with the home's architecture, these lanterns bring light—not glare—to the space. Fixture from Historic Lighting.

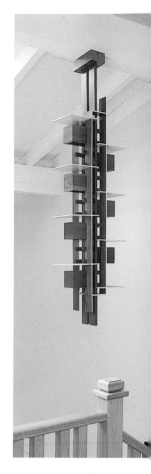

Sconces either act as art or they work with the art in wall arrangements.

Ceiling-hung lighting runs the gamut between decorative and task lighting. A variety of styles are suitable for the bungalow, from Frank Lloyd Wright or Tiffany-type designs to much simpler forms. All lighting on this page is from Historic Lighting.

SCONCES

Sconces are often considered directional lighting. They are meant to greet people in the entry or grand hall and then lead them into the living room, where sconces often frame the fireplace over the mantel. In the dining room they draw attention to the server or sideboard. They are also used in stairwells and halls. They are often the first light you turn on once you enter the bedroom. In bathrooms they frame the mirror over the sink area.

PENDANTS, CHANDELIERS, AND CEILING MOUNTS

Pendants, chandeliers, or ceiling mounts run the gamut between decorative and task lighting. Entries, parlors, and dining rooms are wonderful venues to decorate with Tiffany-style chandeliers or table and floor lamps. Pendants are also used in hallways and kitchen work areas. There is also the infamous plain bulb fixture, the turn-of-the-twentieth-century's answer to today's recess canned lighting. The works of Tiffany and Greene & Greene add another dimension to recessed lighting by disguising them beautifully with glass panels framed with carved wood or metal.

RECESSED AND TRACK LIGHTING

Although their appropriateness for historic-model bungalows is often controversial, these contemporary light sources can be used in new bungalow–style homes and offices. It is important to remember that their roles are to take the eyes away from these sources of light and direct them toward what is decorative. One of the ways to accomplish this is with period light fixtures, originals, or reproductions.

Recessed and track lighting play an important part in fulfilling the demands that our lifestyles require. They provide lighting under, over, and within cabinetry to bring ambiance to the setting. Strip lighting, as it sometimes is referred to, can be used along beams or within soffits, again bringing indirect light into a room.

TODAY'S ADVANCES

There is nothing wrong with the advances we have made in lighting. The problems occur when taste and design are sacrificed. It is this author's opinion that if Morris, Stickley, Wright, Tiffany, Van Erp, and Charles and Henry Greene were here today, they would embrace what is presently available and find more to work with to enhance their creations.

The passion for this revival is strong. The craftsmen and artisans of this century have embraced the work of this period's original craftsmen and artisans and are adding to it. Their attention to detail, return to simpler designs, and commitment to the art are what fuel this renaissance.

Whether you want to go with a full-out bungalow period-style home, or whether you just want to incorporate some elements that would give you the feeling of a bungalow and make your house unique, these ideas and examples have shown how you can do it.

: INTERPRETING : :

THE SPIRIT

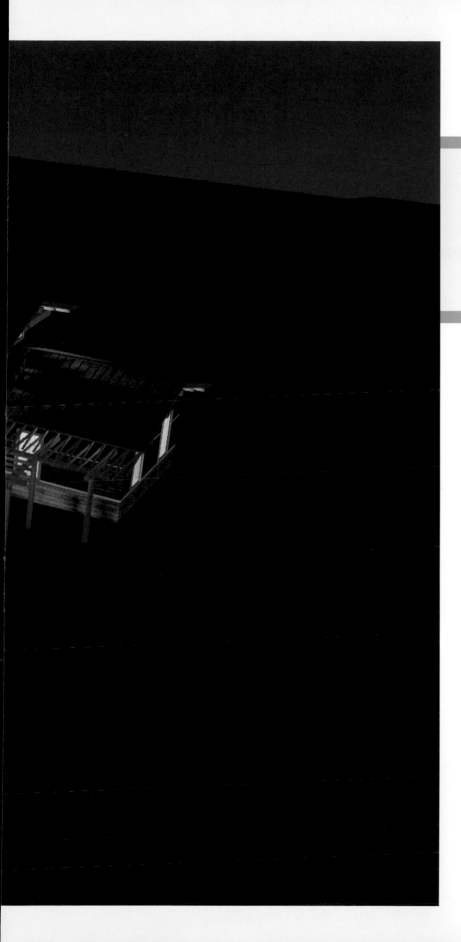

Matthew Bialecki, AIA

Arts & Crafts is so young . . . let's learn what the masters did, learn how they did it, and then adapt it to the landscape and your own expression. That will make it new and exciting, every time.

—*Matthew Bialecki, AIA, quoted in* **Period Homes**

The new bungalow, the residential design that will take us happily to the doors of the next millennium, is not a copy of a Stickley craftsman or a Greene & Greene masterwork. Pieces of it, however, are to be seen here and there, giving glimmers of hope that show a growing awareness of new problems that need new solutions while embracing the fundamentals of the bungalow movement: honest straightforward design ✦ unrefined natural materials used directly ✦ exposed structure as a primary design

Aerial view of the courtyard and gardens of the Vidich-Stein house in High Falls, New York. Matthew Bialecki, architect.

element ✦ a direct relationship to the landscape ✦ affordability and practicality for our lives today. Nature-based design is an appropriate label because its fundamental statement is about a harmony with the land, our communities, and our place in them.

View from pool showing breakfast room, sun room, and master bedroom of the Vidich-Stein house. The rooms are arranged informally about the pool area. Matthew Bialecki, architect.

Southwest elevation showing pergola intersecting glass wall of the living room, Vidich-Stein house.

The northwest elevation of the Vidich-Stein house shows the front entry courtyard.

South elevation, Knecht residence, Matthew Bialecki, architect. A screened porch transitions between outdoors and indoor living space.

East view of the Knecht house reveals a pergola that extends living space to the outdoors.

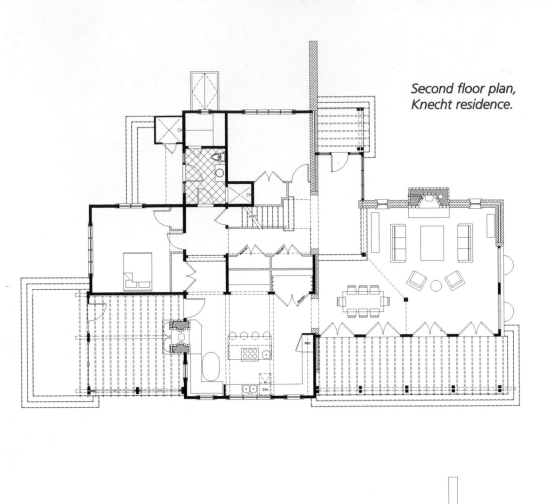

*Second floor plan,
Knecht residence.*

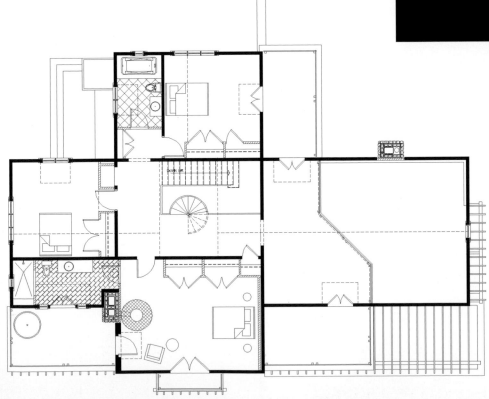

*First-floor plan,
Knecht residence.*

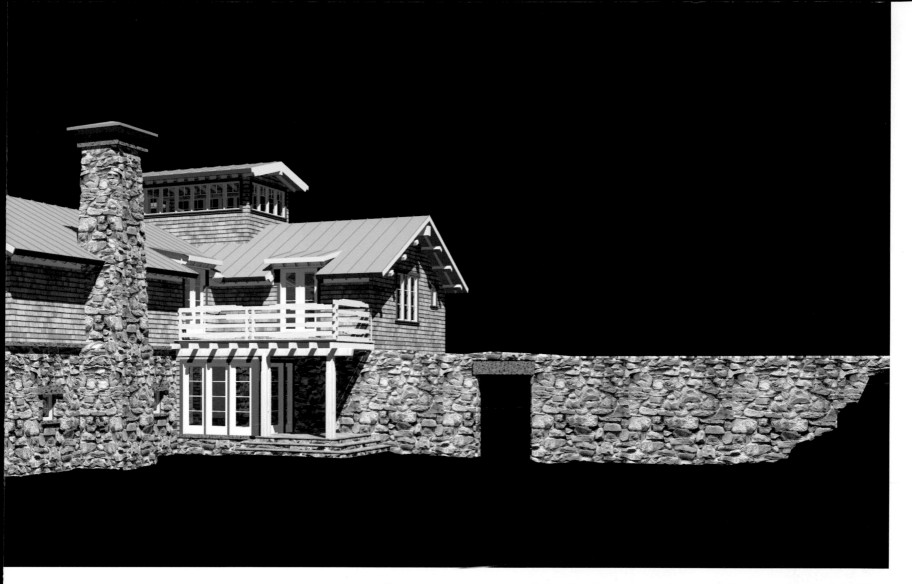

The northwest elevation of the Knecht residence shows another entry porch. An eroded stone wall blends the materials of the house into the landscape.

What are some of today's problems that need innovative solutions? Sustainability heads the list. There wasn't a lot of concern for managing our resources or saving energy back in the early bungalow days. Photovoltaic panels (BIPV's) integrated as roof shingles, strict solar orientation for maximum passive-energy efficiency, earth berming and green roofing for a new type of volumetric massing for the architecture are some workable solutions. Using local sustainable-yield woods, indigenous materials like rammed earth, adobe, straw bale, and other regionally based construction systems are opening new chapters for bungalow design.

One of my favorite architects of all, the San Francisco Bay Area regionalist Bernard Maybeck (1862–1957) was always experimenting with different materials—concrete as finished walls, plywood panels and burlap dipped in plaster for interior wall panels. His work was constantly changing as he tried new forms and nontraditional materials. With the vast range of materials available, the only thing limiting the possibilities of the new bungalow movement is our imagination and willingness to take the risks.

Affordability is a problem that needs addressing. In many regions, nicely built "new" bungalows cost an average of $250–300 per square foot in construction costs alone. This means these homes are affordable to the very few. To be true to its roots, the new bungalow movement needs builder, developer, and architect to team up and develop affordable, nature-based, sustainable designs that can implement the fundamental concepts of a new bungalow for a wider audience. These homes will never be low-income housing, but as historical revival (including some Arts & Crafts revival developments and bungalow developments featured in this book) and as interpretations of the underlying principles, new bungalows have the potential to not only enhance the look of our homes but to unite us in communities around some life-impacting causes.

A major part of affordability is the size and scale of a house. Greene & Greene's ultimate bungalows look positively small next to the typical high-end mansions that fill our well-off neighborhoods today. One of the enduring qualities of the bungalow is its modesty of scale. Big is not beautiful and the unattractiveness of some overblown "mansionettes" is appalling.

Finally, building locally and embracing indigenous materials will help us celebrate the qualities of the regions where we live. In the Southwest, adobe, or rammed earth, or autoclaved concrete are sustainable indigenous materials. In the Northwest, salvaged or recycled woods can fill the bill. Each region has its own characteristic materials and techniques that bring a unique quality to any new nature-based home.

(Opposite) Designs by Matthew Bialecki utilize earthy materials as well as visual representations of nature to augment a nature-based design in an urban space.

There are award-winning architects practicing whose work embodies many of the principles of the bungalow movement. James Cutler and Miller/Hull Architects in the Seattle area do beautifully detailed homes that capture the essence of their region and a new bungalow ideal.

In the Southwest, William Bruder merges raw materials and a strong integration with the landscape to stunning effect. In Texas, Lake/Flato architects have developed a regional courtyard style based on Texas vernacular that incorporates sustainable and recycled materials. In Maine, Peter Forbes has elevated the small gabled structure to high art. In Pennsylvania, Bohlin Cywinski Jackson architects have interpreted historic Adirondack traditions in a way that is not sentimental or coy.

Furniture is integrated into the architecture at 108 Fifth Avenue. Matthew Bialecki, architect.

Ultimately, using nature and landscape as inspiration continues the tradition that began when A. W. Pugin commenced his quest for an honest expression of materials and craftsmanship. The design of the new bungalow will always be fresh and vital if it responds to its site and the particular conditions surrounding it. Don't chop the tree down; build a building around it. Don't remove the boulders; build the fireplace with them. Above all, bring the sun in—east, west, south, country or urban sites. Use the light and celebrate it.

Study and learn from the local building traditions and available materials. These principles are as valid today as they were 150 years ago; we just have to keep applying them to problems we face today. The solutions we find will keep the bungalow unique and fresh for the next millennium.

A cast-aluminum basin sits atop the counter in a design by Matthew Bialecki.

: HOME SHOW :
OF DETAILS

In an effort to honor the Arts & Crafts ideal of fusing architecture with nature, Highland Group incorporated local river rock in the construction of this new bungalow. Shawn Wright was the mason. The roofing is natural cedar shakes, and the walls are cedar shingles laid in a pattern specified by Tim and Tim of Highland Group. Copper rain gutters and fascias are in keeping with the bungalow tradition.

Tin ceiling tiles bring old style and new character to this dining area. Photo courtesy David Papazian.

These Greene & Greene–style staircase details were fashioned by owner/builder Pat Qualey. Courtesy of Historic Lighting.

Natural elements like this fireplace stonework bring a softer feel to the contemporary style of this home. Courtesy of Historic Lighting.

This beam-and-purlin ceiling designed by Matthew Bialecki is illuminated with copper-and-mica fixtures by Michael Adams of Aurora Studios.

The Wrightian tree motif seen in these ceramic fireplace tiles was repeated throughout the house. Tiles designed by Simply Fetched.

These Frank Lloyd Wright–inspired lines are brought to life with a Tiffany-style chandelier from Historic Lighting.

This adventurous mahogany bed designed by Matthew Bialecki for the Studley house is held together with iron straps that are locked with clasps and opposing wedges while the feet sit on slabs of granite.

*Fine Arts & Crafts-
style reproduction
furniture is a viable
alternative to expen-
sive period originals.
This chair, side table,
and lamp are by
Voorhees Craftsman.*

(Far left) The exquisite design and woodwork in the Jacobs house are comparable to the quality of Charles and Henry Greene. Gilbert Lee Hershberger, architect.

Painting detail on a door designed by Matthew Bialecki, AIA.

(Right) This pergola by Curtis Gelotte and Associates is a romantic blending of the outside and inside.

A mahogany end table in the Studley house is designed by Matthew Bialecki and reflects his goal of transforming furniture into small works of architecture. Lamp design by Michael Adams.

Two-tone paint applied to the columns throughout the Mangelson house accentuates the details. Ambient lighting reflects off the ceiling and lifts the structure.

:RESOURCES:

ARTS & CRAFTS STYLE

Organizations/Places

Arts & Crafts Society
1194 Bandera Dr
Ann Arbor MI 48103
(734) 665-4729
(734) 661-2883 fax
Info@arts-crafts.com

Craftsman Farms
2352 Rte 10-West #5
Morris Plains NJ 07950
(973) 540-1165
(973) 540-1167 fax
Craftsmanfarms@att.net

The Gamble House
4 Westmoreland Pl
Pasadena CA 91103
(626) 793-3334
gamblehs@usc.edu

Books from Gibbs Smith, Publisher

Baca, Elmo. *Romance of the Mission,* 1996.

Cigliano, Jan, and Walter Smalling Jr. (photos). *Bungalow: American Restoration Style,* 1998.

Ewald, Chase Reynolds. *Arts and Crafts Style and Spirit: Craftspeople of the Revival,* 1999.

Heinz, Thomas A. *Frank Lloyd Wright's Stained Glass & Lightscreens,* 2000.

Makinson, Randell L. *Greene & Greene: Architecture as a Fine Art* (1977) / *Greene & Greene: Furniture and Related Designs* (1979), 2-in-1 pb, 2001.

Makinson, Randell L., Thomas A. Heinz, and Brad Pitt (photo essay). *Greene & Greene: The Blacker House,* 2000.

Makinson, Randell L. *Greene & Greene: The Passion and the Legacy,* 1998.

Powell, Jane, and Linda Svendsen (photos). *Bungalow Bathrooms,* 2001.

Powell, Jane, and Linda Svendsen (photos). *Bungalow Kitchens,* 2000.

Smith, Bruce, and Yoshiko Yamamoto. *The Beautiful Necessity: Decorating with Arts & Crafts,* 1996.

Varnum, William Harrison. *Arts & Crafts Design,* reprint 1995.

Wallace, Ann, and Phil Bard (photos). *Arts & Crafts Textiles,* 1999.

Yamamoto, Yoshiko, Bruce Smith, and Gail Yngve. *Arts & Crafts Ideals: Wisdom from the Arts & Crafts Movement in America,* 1999.

ARCHITECTS, BUILDERS & PLANNING CONSULTANTS

Tim Andersen, Architect
Seattle, WA
(206) 524-8841
Pasadena, California
(626) 793-4914
timsen@seanet.com

Ashmore/Kessenich Design
6336 NE Garfield Ave
Portland OR 97211
(503) 286-6258

Ashmore/Kessenich Design
Madison, WI
(608) 233-0354

Su Bacon
Historic Lighting, Inc.
114 East Lemon Ave
Monrovia CA 91016
(626) 303-4899
(626) 358-6159 fax
www.historiclighting.com

Bainbridge Island Bungalow Company
4890 Taylor Ave
Bainbridge Island WA 98110
(206) 842-7910
(206) 727-6352 fax

Baylis Architects
10801 Main St, Ste 110
Bellevue, WA 98004
(425) 454-0566

BC Mountain Homes
501-622 Front St
Nelson BC
Canada V1L 4B7
(250) 352-2502 ph/fax

Kurt Beckmeyer
Beckmeyer Carver Architects
1151 El Centro, Ste E
South Pasadena, CA 91030
(626) 799-2277

Matthew Bialecki Associates
108 Main St
New Paltz, NY 12561
(914) 255-6131
(914) 255-6276 fax

Blankemeyer & Blankemeyer
1409 W Third Ave
Columbus OH 43212
(614) 488-7263
(614) 488-7264 fax
Amerfurn@aol.com

The Bungalow Company
550 SW Industrial Way, Ste 37
Bend OR 97702
(541) 312-2674
(877) 785-7512 fax
thebungalowcompany.com

Castlerock Homes, Inc.
347 NW 83rd Pl
Portland, OR 97229
(503) 292-2819
www.castlerock-home-inc.com

Circa Design
1376 Yosemite Ave
San Jose CA 95126
(408) 998-1906
(408) 998-2545 fax

Juidiith Clawson
Simply Fetched
2257 South 1100 East
Salt Lake City, UT 84105
(801) 468-0526
www.simplyfetched.com

Michael Colombo, AIA
JTS Architects
101 Schelter Rd
Lincolnshire, IL 60069-3603
(847) 634-8100
www.jtsarch.com

Marshall Compton
4980 Miami Rd
Cincinnati OH 45243
(513) 784-1234
(513) 561-2312 fax

Charles Cook
Myefski Cook Architects
Glencoe, IL
(847) 835-7081

Michael Corcoran, Architect
Corcoran & Corcoran
2240 University Dr, Ste 120
Newport Beach, CA 92660
(949) 650-0600

Eagan & Associates, Architects
8116 Old York Rd
Elkins Park, PA 19001
(215) 635-2600

Felhandler, Steeneken, and Wilk, Architects
151 West 85th St #4
New York NY 10024
(800) 791-9522
(212) 874-6277 fax
Info@fswarchitects.com

Curtis Gelotte
150 Lake St South, Ste 208
Kirkland WA 98033
(425) 828-3081
(425) 822-2512 fax

Genesis Architecture
6929 Mariner Dr, Ste C
Racine WI 53406
(262) 886-6656
(262) 886-6657 fax

Greene & Proppe Design Inc.
1209 West Berwyn Ave
Chicago IL 60640
(773) 271-1925
(773) 271-1936 fax

William East Hamilton Designs
6701 Mallards Cove Rd #39F
Jupiter FL 33458
(561) 743-7657
(561) 746-6429 fax

David Heide Design
301 4th Ave S, Ste 663
Minneapolis, MN 55415
(612) 337-5060
www.davidheidedesign.com

Gilbert Lee Hershberger
1471 Indiana Ave
South Pasadena, CA 91030
(323) 256-2526

Highland Group
Tim Wyatt and Tim Furner
4471 South Highland Dr
Salt Lake City, UT 84124
(801) 277-4433
(801) 277-1450 fax
Tims@highland-group.com
www.highland-group.com

Hoyle, Doran & Berry, Inc.
38 Newbury St
Boston, MA 02116
(617) 424-6200
(617) 424-7762 fax

The Johnson Partnership
1212 NE 65th St
Seattle WA 98115-6724
(206) 523-1618

JSA
John Shirley, Architect
3115 Lion Ln #300
Salt Lake City, UT 84121
(801) 278-8151
(801) 278-8661 fax

A. Kitsinger, AIA
1665 Overton Park Ave
Memphis TN 38112
(901) 272-0155

Robert Lidsky
The Hammer & Nail
232 Madison Ave
Wyckoff, NJ 07481
(201) 891-5252

Johan Luchsinger
Baylis Architects
10801 Main St, Ste 110
Bellevue, WA 98004
(425) 454-0566

John Malick and Associates
1195 Park Ave, Ste 102
Emeryville, CA 94608
(510) 595-8042

Marcus and Willers, Architects
415 First St West, Ste 3
Sonoma CA 95476
(707) 996-2396 ph/fax

Alan Mascord Design
Associates
1305 NW 18th Ave
Portland, OR 97209
(800) 411-0231
(503) 225-0933 fax
www.mascord.com

Jim McCord
503 Wave St
Monterey, CA 93940-1426
(831) 375-7800
(831) 655-3259 fax

New Urbanist Homes
St. Charles, MO
(636) 688-7111
info@newurbanist.com

Prairie Architects, Inc.
103 South Third St
Fairfield IA 52556
(515) 472-9981

Preservation + Planning
1382 Perry Ave
Salt Lake City UT 84103
(801) 814-5405
(801) 355-8611 fax

Princeton Plans Press
PO Box 622
Princeton NJ 08540
(609) 924-9655
(800) 566-9655 toll-free

Spencer Ruff Associates, Inc.
732 East Woodlawn Dr
Sioux Falls SD 57105
(605) 331-5413
(605) 331-2101 fax

SALA Architects, Inc.
43 Main St SE, Ste 410
Minneapolis MN 55414
(612) 379-3037
(612) 379-0001 fax
www.salaarch.com

Salmon Falls Architecture
56 Industrial Park Road, Ste #7
Saco MA 04072
(207) 283-4247
(207) 284-4546 fax

Les Schulz, Architect
1664 East Grand
Springfield MO 65804
(417) 863-8448
(417) 863-0131 fax

David M. Schwarz /
Architectural Services Inc
1701 L St NW, Ste 400
Washington, DC 20036
(202) 862-0777
Fax (202) 331-0507
www.dmsas.com

Simply Fetched
Juidiith Clawson
2257 South 1100 East
Salt Lake City, UT 84105
(801) 468-0526
www.simplyfetched.com

Spellman Construction
8509 Ferncliff Ave
Bainbridge Island, WA 98110
(206) 842-2786
spellcon@jps.net

CRAFTSMEN

Associations

Western Red Cedar Lumber
Association
1200 - 555 Burrard St
Vancouver BC
Canada V7X 1S7
(604) 684-0266
(604) 687-4930 fax
wrcla@wrcla.org

Window and Door
Manufacturers Association
1400 East Touhy Ave, Ste 470
Des Plaines IL 60018
(800) 223-2301
(847) 299-1286 fax
admin@wdma.com

Building Links

Energy & Environmental
Building Association
10740 Lyndale Ave S, Ste 10W
Bloomington MN 55420-5615
(952) 881-1098
(952) 881-3048 fax
info@eeba.org

National Association of
Home Builders
400 Prince George's Blvd
Upper Marlboro MD 20774
(301) 249-4000
(800) 638-8556 toll-free
(301) 430-6180 fax

Building Products

American Timbers LLC
PO Box 430
Canterbury CT 06331
(800) 461-8660
(860) 546-9334 fax

Artwood Design
10-755 Vanalman Ave
Victoria BC
Canada V8Z 3B8
(250) 727-3100
(250) 727-7887 fax

Custom Hardwoods
1030 Wild St
Sycamore IL 60178
(815) 895-9519
(815) 895-7493 fax

Dowd Stonemasonry
RR1 Box 108
Barre MA 01005
(978) 355-6396

Eco-Timber Ltd.
175 Pitt St
Saint John NB
Canada E2L 2W8
(506) 642-9663
(506) 657-5100 fax

Extraordinary Doors
953 C Tower Pl
Santa Cruz CA 95062
(831) 465-1470
(813) 465-1471 fax

Grabill Inc.
Windows and Doors
7463 Research Dr
Almont MI 48003
(810) 798-2817
(810) 798-2809 fax

Historic Home Supply
Corporation
213–215 River St
Troy NY 12180-3809
(518) 266-0675
(518) 266-0810 fax

Livos Natural Wood Finishes
PO Box 1740
800 Falmouth Road
Mashpee MA 02649
(508) 477-7955
(508) 477-7988 fax

McGrory Glass, Inc.
100 Commerce Dr
Aston PA 19014
(800) 220-3749 toll-free
(610) 364-1071 fax

Prairie Woodworking
343 Harrison St
Oak Park IL 60304
(708) 386-0603 ph/fax

Remanufactured Hardwoods
2630 Loop 35
Alvin TX 77511
(281) 331-7838
(381) 331-6467 fax

Superior Water-Logged Lumber
2200 East Lakeshore Dr
Ashland WI 54806
(715) 685-9663
(715) 685-9620 fax

Talarico Hardwoods
RD 3, Box 3268
Mohnton PA 19540
(610) 775-0400
(610) 775-1456 fax

Woodshed
2505 - 12th Ave South
Moorhead MN 56560
(218) 236-0009

Fireplaces

The Chimney Pot Shoppe
Michael Bentley Enterprise
Avella PA 15312
(724) 345-3601
bentley@chimneypot.net

Heat-N-Glo—A Division of
Hearth Technologies
20802 Kensington Blvd
Lakeville MN 55044
(888) 743-2887

Vermont Castings
Majestic Products
410 Admiral Blvd
Mississauga ON
Canada L5T 2N6

Market Places

The Craftsman Home
3048 Claremont Ave
Berkeley, CA 94705
(510) 655–6503
lee@craftsmanhome.com

The Craftsman Homes
Collection
PMB 343
2525 East 29th, Ste 10B
Spokane, WA 99223
(509) 535-5098
(509) 534-8916
Elvis@crafthome.com

Siding

Builder Online
One Thomas Circle NW
Ste 600
Washington DC 20005
(202) 452-0800
(202) 785-1974 fax
www.builderonline.com

Cedar Shake & Shingle Bureau
PO Box 1178
Sumas WA 98295-1178
(604) 820-7700
(604) 820-0266 fax

Tile

Claystone
547-B Constitution Ave
Camarillo CA 93012
(805) 388-5248
(805) 388-7298 fax
brahma@claystone.com

Ephraim Faience
Bookfield, WI
(800) 704-POTS [7687]
    toll-free

Motawi Tile Works
33 North Staebler, Ste 2
Ann Arbor, MI 48103
(734) 213-0017
(734) 213-2569 fax
motawi@bizserve.com

Norberry Tile
207 Second Ave South
Seattle WA 98104
(206) 343-9916
(206) 343-9917 fax

Tile Restoration Center
3511 Interlake North
Seattle WA 98103
(206) 633-4866
trc@wolfenet.com

Windows

Andersen Commercial Group
PO Box 12
100 Fourth Ave North
Bayport MN 55003-1096
(800) 299-9029
    (U.S. and Canada)
(651) 264-5279 fax
commercialgroup@
    andersenwindows.com

Efficient Windows
Collaborative Alliance
to Save Energy
1200 -18th St NW, Ste 900
Washington DC 20036
(202) 530-2245
(202) 331-9588
www.ase.org

Excell
(stained glass)
via Juidiith Clawson
Simply Fetched
2257 South 1100 East
Salt Lake City, UT 84105
(801) 468-0526
www.simplyfetched.com

Wood Products

Bear Creek Lumber
PO Box 669
Winthrop WA 98862
(800) 597-7191 toll-free
(509) 997-2040 fax

Boise Cascade
Engineered Wood Products

Corporate Headquarters
PO Box 50
Boise ID 83728-0001
(800) 232-0788 toll-free
(208) 384-7455 fax
info@BCEWP.com

Crosscut Hardwood—Eugene
2344 West 7th Pl
Eugene OR 97402
(541) 349-0538

Crosscut Hardwood—Portland
3065 NW Front Ave
Portland OR 97210
(503) 224-9663
(503) 227-4670 fax

Crosscut Hardwoods—Seattle
4100 First Ave South
Seattle WA 98134
(206) 623-0334
(800) 756-0334 toll-free
(206) 623-0556 fax

TimberGrass LLC
9790 Murden Cove Dr
Bainbridge Island WA 98110
(206) 842-9477
(800) 929-6333 toll-free
(206) 842-9818 fax
www.timbergrass.com
info@timbergrass.com

HOME CONTRACTORS & RENOVATORS

Artwood Design (Canada) Ltd.
10-755 Vanalman Ave
Victoria BC
Canada V8Z 3B8
(604) 727-3100

Screen Scenes
PO Box 3625
Quincy CA 95971
(530) 283-4366
(530) 283-4675 fax
Scrnscns@inreach.com

GARDENS & LANDSCAPING

Arto Brick/California Pavers
3751 Durango Ave
Los Angeles CA 90034
(940) 591-0518 ph/fax

W. D. Bosworth Woodworking
59 Luther Warren Dr
St. Helena Island SC 29920
(843) 838-9490
(843) 838-1187 fax
Woodwork@hargray.com

Copper Forge
2148 Inner Circle Dr
Rockford IL 61101
(815) 965-5314

Rick Darke
526 Chambers Rock Rd
Landenberg PA 19350
(610) 255-0432
(610) 255-0439 fax

Richard Liberto
1907 Lowrie St
Pittsburgh PA 15212-3224
(412) 321-4427 ph/fax

Old House Gardens
536 West Third St
Ann Arbor MI 48103-4957
(734) 995-1486
(734) 995-1687 fax

INTERIOR DECORATORS & DESIGNERS

Juidiith Clawson
Simply Fetched
2257 South 1100 East
Salt Lake City, UT 84105
(801) 468-0526
www.simplyfetched.com

Distinctions Interior
Consultation Services
235 Summit View Cove
Collierville TN 38017
(901) 484-2397

Highland Group
Valerie Paoli-Johnson and
Rebecca Osborne
4471 South Highland Dr
Salt Lake City, UT 84124
(801) 277-4433
(801) 277-1450 fax
www.highland-group.com

Interior Vision in the
Craftsman Style
PO Box 867
Port Townsend WA 98368
(360) 385-3161
(888) 385-3161 toll-free
(360) 385-4874 fax

INTERIORS

Cabinetry

Acorn (Forged Iron)
Mansfield, MA
(800) 835-0121

Crown City (Arts & Crafts)
Pasadena, CA
(800) 950-1047 toll-free

Crownpoint Cabinetry
153 Charlestown Road
Claremont NH 03743
(800) 999-4994
    toll-free phone
(800) 370-1218 toll-free fax
www.crown-point.com

Crystal
Princeton, MN
(612) 389-4240

Designer Doors Inc.
283 Troy St
River Falls WI 54022
(715) 426-1100
(800) 241-0525 toll-free
info@designerdoors.com

Gainsborough
(Turn of the Century)
Norcross, GA
(800) 845-5662 toll-free

International Door & Latch
191 Seneca Rd
PO Box 25755
Eugene OR 97402
(541) 686-5647
(888) 686-3667 toll-free
(541) 686-4166 fax
www.internationaldoor.com

Notting Hill
Lake Geneva, WI
(414) 248-8890

William Russell Doors
31 Doornang Rd
Scoresby, Victoria
3179 Australia
(03) 9763 1544
(03) 9764 2250 fax
www.wrusselldoors.com

Rutt of Seattle
Seattle, WA
(206) 762-2603

Furniture & Frames

CRAFTSMEN

Holton
Emeryville, CA
(800) 250-5277 toll-free

Troy Poulson
Millcreek Furniture
via Simply Fetched
2257 S 1100 E
Salt Lake City, UT 84105
(801) 468-0526
www.simplyfetched.com

Sandhill Designs
Morrisonville, Wisconsin
(608) 846-2717

Voorhees Craftsman
Rohnert Park, CA
(888) 982-6377 toll-free

REFINISHING & REPAIR

Restoration & Design Studio
249 East 77th St
New York NY 10021
(212) 517-9742

Hardware

Chown Hardware
PO Box 2888
333 NW 16th Ave
Portland, OR 97208
(503) 243-6500
(800) 547-1930 toll-free
(503) 243-6519 fax
(800) 758-7654 toll-free fax
www.chown.com

Craftsmen Hardware Co., Ltd.
PO Box 161
Marceline MO 64658
(660) 376-2481
(660) 376-4076 fax

Crown City Hardware
1047 North Allen Ave
Pasadena CA 91104-3292
(626) 794-1188
(626) 794-0234 catalog direct
(800) 816-8492
    toll-free/orders only
questions@
    crowncityhardware.com

Hahn's Woodworking
Company, Inc.
109 Aldene Rd, Bldg #8
Roselle NJ 07203
(908) 241-8825
(908) 241-9293 fax
info@hahnswoodworking.com

Hippo Hardware
1040 East Burnside St
Portland OR 97214
(503) 231-1444
www.hipponet.com

Lighting

Brass Light Gallery
Milwaukee, WI
(800) 243-9595 toll-free

Historic Lighting, Inc.
114 East Lemon Ave
Monrovia CA 91016
(626) 303-4899
(626) 358-6159 fax
www.historiclighting.com

Luminaria Lighting
South 154 Madison
Spokane WA 99201
(509) 747-9198
(800) 638-5619 toll-free
info@luminarialighting.com

Old California Lantern
Company
975 North Enterprise
Orange CA 92867
(714) 771-5714
(800) 577-6679 toll-free

Rejuvenation House Parts
Portland, Oregon
(888) 3GETLIT [343-8548] toll-free

Rejuvenation Lamp
& Fixture Co.
2550 NW Nicolai St
Portland OR 97210
(503) 231-1900

(888) 401-1900 toll-free
(503) 230-0537 fax
(800) 526-7329 toll-free fax
info@rejuvenation.com

Plumbing & Faucets

Affordable Antique
Baths & More
San Andreas, CA
(209) 754-1797

Ann Sacks
5 East 16th St
New York, NY 10003
(212) 463-8400
(212) 463-0067 fax
www.annsacks.com

Restoration Hardware
104 Challenger Dr
Portland TN 37148-1703
Home office:
    Corte Madera CA 94925
(800) 762-1005
    toll-free customer service
(888) 243-9720
    toll-free information
www.RestorationHardware.com
—Sinks, tubs, faucets, lighting, Mission-style furniture.

Sign of the Crab
Chicago Faucet
A-Ball Plumbing
Portland, OR
(503) 228-0026

The Sink Factory
2140 San Pablo Ave
Berkeley CA 94702
(510) 540-8193
(510) 540-8212 fax
TheCrew@sinkfactory.com
www.sinkfactory.com
—Pre-1940s reproduction
sinks, tubs, and faucets.

Textiles:
Drapes/Carpeting

Dianne Ayers
Arts & Crafts Period Textiles
5427 Telegraph Ave, Ste W2
Oakland, CA 94709
(510) 654-1645
—Finished textiles, custom
embroidery, applique/embroi-
dery, kits, yardage, hardware.

J. R. Burrows and Company
PO Box 522
Rockland MA 02370
(800) 347-1795 toll-free
www.burrows.com
—Candace Wheeler reproduction textiles, net and jacquard
lace curtains, also carpets.

Ann Chaves
Inglenook Textiles
240 North Grand Ave
Pasadena CA 91103
(mail contact only)
—Custom embroidery.

Heartland House Designs
741 North Oak Park Ave
Oak Park IL 60302
(708) 383-2278
—Frank Lloyd Wright and
Charles Rennie Mackintosh
designs in counted cross-
stitch.

JAX Arts & Crafts Rugs
Berea, KY
(606) 986-5410

Liberty Valances
782 North Fair Oaks Ave
Pasadena CA 91103
(949) 766-7505
(949) 766-3287 fax
Bernie@LibertyValances.com
Attn: Sharon Robinson
    or Bernie Ennis

Michael Fitzsimmons
Decorative Arts
311 West Superior St
Chicago IL 60610
(312) 787-0496
—Reproduction and
antique/finished textiles,
applique/embroidery, also rugs.

Sanderson and Sons
979 Third Ave
New York NY 10022
—William Morris textiles
(to the trade).

Schumacher and Company
939 Third Ave
New York NY 10022
(212) 415-3909
—Frank Lloyd Wright textiles
and carpets (to the trade).

Textile Art Artifacts
1847 Fifth St
Manhattan Beach CA 90266
(310) 379-0207
—Specialist in antique Arts
& Crafts textiles,
applique/embroidery.

Textile Artifacts
12589 Crenshaw Blvd
Hawthorne CA 90250
(310) 676-2424
—Antique and
reproduction fabrics.

Trustworth Studios
Box 1109
Plymouth MA 02362
(508) 746-1847
—Custom needlepoint/kits.

United Crafts
127 West Putnam Ave
Greenwich CT 06830
(203) 869-4898
www.ucrafts.com
—Finished textiles, also rugs.

Ann Wallace & Friends
Prairie Textiles
Box 2344
Venice CA 90294
(213) 617-3310
www.webmonger.com/
    annwallace/
—Custom window treatments,
finished textiles, yardage, hardware, applique/embroidery.

Wall Finishes

Faux Finishes
Lisa Lacaden and
Mary June Papazian
Portland, Oregon
(503) 335-3131
(503) 291-1415

Fulper Glazes
New Hope, Pennsylvania
(215) 862-3358

WALLPAPER—HANDPRINTED

Bradbury & Bradbury
Benecia, CA
(707) 746-1900

J. R. Burrows and Company
PO Box 522
Rockland MA 02370
(800) 347-1795 toll-free
www.burrows.com
—Candace Wheeler reproduction textiles, net and jacquard
lace curtains, also carpets.

STENCILS/PAINT

Helen Foster Stencils
Sanford, ME
(207) 490-2625

Old-Fashioned Milk Paint
Broton, MA
(508) 448-6336

RESTORATION & PRESERVATION

Consultants

JM Young Furniture Research
& Consulting
376 West 4th St
Elmira NY 14901-2471
(607) 734-3664

Contractors & Services

Burma Design Antique
Restoration
285 Washington St
Union Square
Somerville MA 02143
(617) 628-2666 ph/fax

Custom Cushions
76 Lively Road
Middle Sackville NS
Canada B4E 3A9
(902) 864-3221

FRW Inc.
1550 Richmond Terrace
Staten Island NY 10310
(718) 442-3781
(718) 273-2239 fax

Hyland Studio
650 Reed St
Santa Clara CA 95050
(408) 748-1806
(408) 748-0160 fax
Mfg@jphc.com

Keith's Furniture Stripping
1108 Hazel Rd
Burlington NC 27215
(336) 229-1290

Noordzee Construction
Company
7-1888 Maple St
Vancouver BC
Canada V6J 3S7
(604) 880-1175
(604) 736-8069 fax

Post Manufacturing
343 Harrison St
Canandaigua NY 14424
(716) 396-1570 ph/fax

Robert Schweitzer
3661 Waldenwood Dr
Ann Arbor MI 48105
(734) 668-0298
robs@umich.edu

Stonehedge Restoration
& Antiques
PO Box 32094
Route 863
Highwater St
Hillsboro VA 20134
(540) 668-6985

Wallpaperguru
PO Box 491243
Los Angeles CA 90049
(310) 281-6298

Rudolph Waros Glass
PO Box 678
#17 South Park Row
Waterford PA 16441
(814) 796-3933
(814) 866-6079 fax

Winterburn Group
PO Box 99
Duntroon ON
Canada L0M 1H0
(705) 445-5911 ph/fax

Photo Credits

Key: T=Top, B=Bottom, R=Right, L=Left

Courtesy of Ashmore/Kessenich Design, photography by Steven Ashmore: 74–79, 84–85, 93

Courtesy of Matthew Bialecki: 6, 25, 30, 31, 128, 131–41, 145, 147–50

Courtesy of The Bungalow Company: 54–55, 58–59, 62–63, 65, 66–67, 70, 82, 83, 117
© Kim Carey of Michael Seidl Photography: 54, 58–59, 62–63, 66–67, 70, 80, 83 TR
© Randy Allbritton: 83 L and BR

Courtesy of Marshall Compton; © Kit Morris: 110, 114

Mikel Covey: 22–23, 38, 73, 75, 77–78, 81, 109, 117, 127, 145, 150

Charles Didcott, Didcott Visions (for David M. Schwarz / Architectural Services Inc.) 38 TR, 90–91, 111, 124 T

Curtis Gelotte Architects, Leavitt Contruction Co., © Land Image: 32–33

© Doug Hill: 60–61, 97, 146

Courtesy of the Highland Group; © Pete Houdeshel, photographer: 38, 48, 90, 100, 107, 115, 116, 119, 126, 140

Courtesy of Historic Lighting, © Jon Edwards, photographer (for Su Bacon and Historic Lighting): 4–5, 35–39, 92, 95, 96, 98, 99, 102, 103, 106, 110, 111, 113, 121, 122, 123, 124, 125, 145, 146

Courtesy Douglas Keister: 8–9, 10, 12, 24, 26, 27, 53, 56-57

Courtesy of John Malick: 14–21, 80, 88, 104, 108, 120

Courtesy of Jim McCord: 54–55

© David Papazian: 69, 76, 94, 95, 114, 144

© Pro Image Photography (for Baylis Architects): 118

Durston Saylor (for Matthew Bialecki Associates): 25, 30, 31, 137, 138, 139

© Linda Svendsen: 13, 45, 47, 50–52, 87